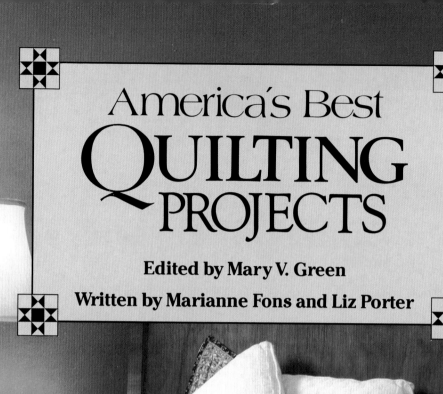

America's Best
QUILTING
PROJECTS

Edited by Mary V. Green

Written by Marianne Fons and Liz Porter

Rodale Press
Emmaus, Pennsylvania

Executive Editor: Margaret Lydic Balitas
Crafts Editor: Suzanne Nelson
Associate Crafts Editor: Mary V. Green
Copy Manager: Dolores Plikaitis
Copy Editor: Sarah S. Dunn
Technical Writers: Marianne Fons and Liz Porter
Administrative assistance: Karen Earl-Braymer and
   Susan Nickol

Art Director: Anita G. Patterson
Cover and Book Designer: Denise M. Shade

Photographer: Mitch Mandel
Illustrator: Ann Nunemacher
Labeler: Robin Hepler
Photo Stylists: Kay Lichthardt and Marianne G. Laubach

On the cover: The quilt shown on the cover is Birthday Tulips and may be found on page 72. The fabric shown on the cover is by St. Nicole Designs for Benartex, Inc.

If you have any questions or comments concerning this book, please write:
   Rodale Press
   Book Readers' Service
   33 East Minor Street
   Emmaus, PA 18098

Library of Congress Cataloging-in-Publication Data

Fons, Marianne.
   America's best quilting projects / written by
Marianne Fons and Liz Porter ; edited by Mary V. Green.
      p.   cm.
   ISBN 0-87596-551-2   hardcover
   1. Patchwork–United States–Patterns.   2. Patchwork quilts–United States.   I. Porter, Liz.   II. Green, Mary V.
III. Title.
TT835.F64   1993
746.46–dc20   92-41508
                                                 CIP

Distributed in the book trade by St. Martin's Press

2   4   6   8   10   9   7   5   3   1   hardcover

Contents

Acknowledgments

East Village Reversals by Nancy Silverman, State College, Pennsylvania. The marriage of her son, Craig, was the event that prompted Nancy to create this quilt. The East Village in the title is the section of New York City where her son and daughter-in-law live; the Reversals part of the title comes from the fact that the colors are reversed in some of the blocks. This quilt was shown at the Quilters' Heritage Celebration in 1990.

Infinity by Linda Harshbarger, Opelika, Alabama. Linda made this quilt as a Christmas gift for her parents. She loves working with prints, especially unusual combinations of prints that present design challenges. Infinity was exhibited at several shows in 1990, including the Quilters' Heritage Celebration.

Amish Nine Patch by Irmgard Stephenson, East Petersburg, Pennsylvania. Encouragement from an Amish friend helped Irmgard make this sparkling quilt. Amish Nine Patch was displayed at the American Quilter's Society show in 1989 and at the Quilters' Heritage Celebration in 1990.

Yankee Barter by Sandra Smith, Killingworth, Connecticut. This quilt is the result of a true barter: Sandra stitched this feathered star variation for her artist friend who, in turn, did an oil painting of Sandra's garden. The quilt was exhibited at the American Quilter's Society show in 1990.

Here's My Heart by Betsy Haney, Midland, Texas. This quilt showcases a combination of techniques, including hand piecing, hand appliqué, and hand quilting with trapunto. The quilt was exhibited at the West Texas Quilt Show in 1989, where it won First Place/Mixed Techniques, and at the Quilters' Heritage Celebration in 1990.

Miniature Iowa Amish Star by Tina M. Gravatt, Philadelphia, Pennsylvania. Tina is a teacher, lecturer, and author whose historically accurate miniatures have appeared in many exhibits and publications. This miniature quilt is based on a circa 1935 pattern.

Patchwork Jewelry Roll by Kathy Berschneider, Rockford, Illinois. Kathy is a quilter and craft designer who has also taught children's quilting classes. This travel roll is her original design.

Blue and White Bed Set by Donna Albert, Lancaster, Pennsylvania. Donna is an award-winning quilt designer whose work has been featured in numerous publications and quilt shows, including the Quilters' Heritage Celebration, the American Quilter's Society show, and the Great American Quilt Festival in New York City. She designed this project as a quick-and-easy decorating option.

Piano Bench Cover by Donna Albert, Lancaster, Pennsylvania. Donna's original design for a cushion cover provides an interesting way to use quilt block patterns as a decorating accent.

Log Cabin Purse Accessories by Donna McConnell, Searcy, Arkansas. Donna is a designer and teacher who publishes her own patterns and markets them nationwide under the name Donna's Designs. She specializes in the use of miniature log cabin blocks to create wallhangings and personal accessories.

Calico Star Room Accessories by Michele Crawford, Spokane, Washington. Michele is a quilt and cross-stitch designer who markets her designs under the name Cross 'n Quilt. Her country-inspired designs have appeared in numerous quilting and crafts magazines.

Country Aprons by Kathy Berschneider, Rockford, Illinois. Kathy designed this project to be quick, fun, and offer lots of options for mixing and matching different designs and colors.

Birthday Tulips by Betty Sale, Kingwood, Texas. Betty spotted this design in a black and white photo in an old quilting magazine, and her husband drafted the pattern for her. The blocks were made with the help of her quilt group, the Cotton Patchers, in honor of Betty's birthday. She designed the setting and the borders and added extensive quilting. This quilt was exhibited at the American Quilter's Society show in 1990.

Amish Fans and Roses by Elsie Schlabach, Millersburg, Ohio. Elsie's quilt, inspired by a nineteenth century design, has won several awards, including Second Place/Amish at the Silver Dollar City show in 1990; Third Place/Pieced at the American Quilt Showcase at Dollywood in Tennessee in 1990; and Best of Show at the Palm Beach Quilt Festival in 1991.

A Walk in the Park by Phyllis Kohler, Racine, Wisconsin. This traditional Boston Commons pattern (not one for the faint of heart) was Phyllis's first quilt! It was exhibited at three shows in 1990: the American Quilter's Society show, the Quilters' Heritage Celebration, and the Wisconsin State Fair, where it won Fourth Place.

Princess Feather and Rose of Sharon by Dana Klein, Dallas, Texas. Inspiration for this quilt came from a photo of an antique quilt in *Quilt Digest 3*. Dana's interpretation of that antique quilt has won several awards, including Second Place/Appliqué at the Dallas Quilt Guild Show in 1989; Second Place/Appliqué/Artisan at the Houston Quilt Festival in 1989; and Second Place/Appliqué and Judges' Choice at the Quilters' Heritage Celebration in 1990.

Spring Garden by Nancy S. Breland, Pennington, New Jersey. Chintz decorator remnants in a fabric store caught Nancy's eye and led to the creation of Spring Garden. This quilt was displayed at the American Quilter's Society show in 1990.

Silverainbow by Adrien Rothschild, Baltimore, Maryland. Adrien is a quilt designer whose work has been seen in numerous shows and publications. The design for this quilt came from a crayon sketch that Adrien made when she was about five years old. Her mother, obviously recognizing her talent, faithfully saved that sketch for years, and Adrien re-created it in fabric. Silverainbow was displayed at the Flight of Imagination quilt show in Ephrata, Pennsylvania, in 1991.

Lilies of the Field by Betty Ekern Suiter, Racine, Wisconsin. Two years in the making, this elaborate quilt is a copy of an 1850 quilt made in New England. Lilies of the Field was exhibited at the Quilters' Heritage Celebration in 1990, at the American Quilter's Society show in 1991, and at the Flight of Imagination quilt show in Ephrata, Pennsylvania, in 1991. Betty has been designated a Master Quilter by the National Quilting Association, one of only ten people to have earned that title.

Here Comes the Sun by Adrien Rothschild, Baltimore, Maryland. The name of this quilt has special meaning for its maker. A medical diagnosis alerted Adrien that she needs to be exposed to sunlight all year round. She designed this quilt as a way to show how the coming of the sun enabled her to move ahead with her quilting career.

Hearts and Vines Table Runner by Lois Reff, Fergus Falls, Minnesota. Lois designed this table runner as a gift for her mother. Besides designing and making quilts and quilt projects, Lois keeps busy teaching adult education classes in quilting and taking part in guild activities.

Something's Fishy by Carolyn Maruggi, Pittsford, New York. A young nephew, Danny, is the lucky recipient of Carolyn's playful, multicolored quilt. The design popped into her head one day while she was reading an article in *Smithsonian* magazine about undersea life.

Holiday Place Mat Set by Michele Crawford, Spokane, Washington. Michele designed these to be fast and fun, in keeping with the spirit of the holidays.

Carnation Carousel by Pat Magaret, Pullman, Washington. In designing this beautiful wallhanging, Pat was inspired by a Judy Martin quilting design in a 1987 issue of *Quilter's Newsletter Magazine.* The quilt was made with a preselected packet of fabrics as part of a guild challenge project. Pat's quilt was exhibited at the American Quilter's Society show in 1990.

Countryside Wreath by Lynette Jensen, Hutchinson, Minnesota. Lynette is a quilt and quilt craft designer who markets her own patterns under the name Thimbleberries. This seasonal wallhanging is just one part of her holiday collection.

Introduction

Quilters love to share. They share knowledge, skills, ideas, and traditions. They exchange fabrics, patterns, and tricks they've learned. And they give generously of themselves: They acknowledge experienced quilters for the fine work they do, and they warmly encourage newcomers to the craft.

Quilt guilds offer a great opportunity for sharing, as do the many classes offered at shops and quilt conferences across the country. We think one of the best forums for sharing is the quilt show. These shows range from small, guild-sponsored shows displaying several dozen quilts, to large, international shows with several hundred quilts. These large shows, including the American Quilter's Society show in Paducah, Kentucky, the Quilters' Heritage Celebration in Lancaster, Pennsylvania, and the International Quilt Festival in Houston, display quilts from around the country and around the world. For the quiltmakers, these large shows offer an opportunity to display their best work and to share their hard work and talent with an audience. For other quiltmakers and quilt lovers, the shows offer a chance to examine, admire, and be inspired by a breathtaking array of bed quilts and wallhangings.

Unfortunately, not every quilt lover has the opportunity to attend a major quilt show. Since we want everyone to experience some of the excitement, we've gone to the shows for you and brought back some of the most beautiful quilts we could find. We traveled throughout the country to assemble this special collection of bed quilts and wallhangings for you to re-create at home. And we've even added some smaller quilted projects for you to enjoy. The total collection of 25 projects represents the best work done by a wonderfully talented group of American quiltmakers.

These projects are a delightful sampling of what's going on in quiltmaking today. Many of them are based on traditional patterns, but with a fresh twist or a unique color approach. There's bound to be something here that will stir your creativity.

Once you've spotted a project (or two or three or more) that you want to make, you'll find that the directions include many features specially tailored to a quiltmaker's needs. Each project features an indication of skill level, a list of all the fabrics and supplies you need, step-by-step directions with lots of diagrams, and full-size patterns so you don't have to waste time with enlargements. At the back of the book, you'll find a Tips and Techniques section, which includes all the general information you need to make a quilt, plus lots of valuable tips and handy ideas to guarantee your project is a success. And in the Acknowledgments section, you can read about the quilts and their makers: what inspired them, where the patterns came from, what shows the quilts have appeared in.

We'd like to thank the quiltmakers for generously sharing their projects with us so that we could bring them to you. We'd also like to thank Meredith Schroeder of the American Quilter's Society and Rita Barber of Barber Diversified, organizer of the Quilters' Heritage Celebration, for their assistance in contacting the quiltmakers. For additional information about these and other quilt shows, please see the Directory of Quilt Shows at the end of the book.

Whether you make 1 project or all 25, you'll love having your own private quilt show collection to page through again and again. Enjoy the show!

Mary Green

Mary V. Green
Project Editor

vii

HEARTH
and
HOME

East Village Reversals

Two traditional quilt blocks—Triangles and Stripes and Double Squares—alternate in this stylish bed quilt. Rearranging the fabrics results in two versions of each block and creates a delightfully subtle pattern of color variations from one end of the quilt to the other. Quick-cutting techniques and simple borders make this quilt fast and easy.

Skill Level: Easy

Size: Finished quilt is 84 × 108 inches
Finished block is 12 inches square

Fabrics and Supplies

- 5½ yards of rose print fabric for blocks, borders, and binding
- 2¾ yards of medium blue print fabric for blocks and borders
- 2¾ yards of light blue print fabric for blocks and borders
- 2½ yards of dark blue print fabric for blocks
- 1¼ yards of pastel blue print fabric for blocks
- 3¼ yards of 90-inch-wide fabric for quilt back
- King-size quilt batting (120 inches square)
- Rotary cutter, ruler, and mat
- Template plastic (optional)

Cutting

These instructions are written for quick-cutting the pattern pieces with a rotary cutter and ruler. Note that for some of the pieces, the quick-cutting method will result in leftover strips of fabric. If you prefer to cut the pieces in a traditional manner, make templates for the following pieces (measurements include ¼-inch seam allowances):

- **A:** Make a 3⅞-inch square; cut the square in half diagonally.
- **B:** 2 × 6½-inch rectangle
- **C:** Make a 3-inch square; cut the square in half diagonally.
- **D:** 3½-inch square
- **E:** 2⅝ × 4¾-inch rectangle
- **F:** 2⅝ × 9-inch rectangle

All measurements include ¼-inch seam allowances. Measurements for the borders are longer than needed; trim them to the exact length as they are added to the quilt top.

From the rose print fabric, cut:
- Two 6½ × 114-inch side strips and two 6½ × 90-inch top and bottom strips for the fourth border

- Two 1½ × 96-inch side strips and two 1½ × 72-inch top and bottom strips for the second border
- 120 A triangles

  Quick-Cutting Method: Cut six 3⅞ × 44-inch strips; cut each strip into 3⅞-inch squares. You will need 60 squares. Cut each square in half diagonally to make two triangles.
- 16 B rectangles

  Quick-Cutting Method: Cut a 6½ × 44-inch strip; cut the strip into 2 × 6½-inch rectangles.
- 18 E rectangles

  Quick-Cutting Method: Cut two 4¾ × 44-inch strips; cut the strips into 2⅝ × 4¾-inch rectangles.
- 18 F rectangles

  Quick-Cutting Method: Cut two 9 × 44-inch strips; cut the strips into 2⅝ × 9-inch rectangles.
- Reserve the remaining fabric for binding

From the medium blue print fabric, cut:
- Two 3½ × 99-inch side strips and two 3½ × 75-inch top and bottom strips for the third border
- 72 C triangles

  Quick-Cutting Method: Cut four 3-inch strips across the width of the fabric (approximately 30 inches after border strips have been cut). Cut each strip into 3-inch squares. You will need 36 squares. Cut each square in half diagonally to make two triangles.
- 68 A triangles

  Quick-Cutting Method: Cut five 3⅞-inch strips across the width of the fabric; cut each strip into 3⅞-inch squares. You will need 34 squares. Cut each square in half diagonally to make two triangles.

From the light blue print fabric, cut:
- Two 2½ × 99-inch side strips and two 2½ × 70-inch top and bottom strips for the first border
- 56 B rectangles

  Quick-Cutting Method: Cut four 6½-inch strips across the width of the fabric (approximately 34 inches after border strips have been cut). Cut each strip into 2 × 6½-inch rectangles.
- 88 A triangles

  Quick-Cutting Method: Cut six 3⅞-inch strips across the width of the fabric; cut each strip into 3⅞-inch squares. You will need 44 squares. Cut each square in half diagonally to make two triangles.

- 16 E rectangles

  Quick-Cutting Method: Cut two 4¾-inch strips across the width of the fabric; cut each strip into 2⅝ × 4¾-inch rectangles.

- 16 F rectangles

  Quick-Cutting Method: Cut two 9-inch strips across the width of the fabric; cut each strip into 2⅝ × 9-inch rectangles.

From the dark blue print fabric, cut:

- 72 B rectangles

  Quick-Cutting Method: Cut four 6½ × 44-inch strips; cut the strips into 2 × 6½-inch rectangles.

- 140 A triangles

  Quick-Cutting Method: Cut seven 3⅞ × 44-inch strips; cut each strip into 3⅞-inch squares. You will need 70 squares. Cut each square in half diagonally to make two triangles.

- 35 D squares

  Quick-Cutting Method: Cut four 3½ × 44-inch strips; cut each strip into 3½-inch squares. You will need 35 squares.

From the pastel blue print fabric, cut:

- 72 A triangles

  Quick-Cutting Method: Cut four 3⅞ × 44-inch strips; cut each strip into 3⅞-inch squares. You will need 36 squares. Cut each square in half diagonally to make two triangles.

- 68 C triangles

  Quick-Cutting Method: Cut three 3 × 44-inch strips; cut each strip into 3-inch squares. You will need 34 squares. Cut each square in half diagonally to make two triangles.

Piecing the Blocks

You will need 18 of Block I (Triangles and Stripes) and 17 of Block II (Double Squares). There are two fabric variations for each block. For Block I, you will need 14 IA and 4 IB blocks. For Block II, you will need 8 IIA and 9 IIB blocks.

Block I

Refer to the **Fabric Key** and **Diagram 1** for fabric placement. Construct the blocks as follows, pressing the seams toward the darker fabrics. The fabric colors given in the directions are for the IA Blocks. Make 14 of these blocks first, then follow the same sequence to make 4 of Block IB, changing the fabrics as shown in **Diagram 1.**

Fabric Key

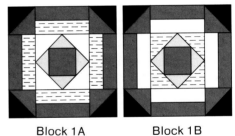

☐ Rose print

☐ Medium blue print

☐ Light blue print

■ Dark blue print

■ Pastel blue print

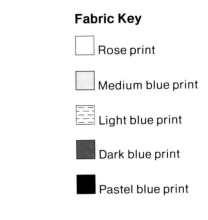

Block 1A   Block 1B

Diagram 1

1. Sew a medium blue C triangle to each side of a D square.

2. Add a rose A triangle to each side of the CD unit to make the center of the block, as shown in **Diagram 2.**

Diagram 2

3. Join a light blue B rectangle to a dark blue B rectangle along the long sides; make four of these BB units.

4. With the light blue toward the center, sew a BB unit to two opposite sides of the center unit, as shown in **Diagram 3.**

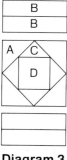

Diagram 3

5. Join a dark blue A triangle to a pastel blue A triangle, forming a square. Make four of these squares.

6. Referring to **Diagram 4** for correct fabric placement, sew a square from Step 5 to each short end of the two remaining BB units.

7. Check to see that the fabrics are positioned correctly, and sew the units from Step 6 to opposite sides of the block, as shown in **Diagram 4.** Make a total of 14 of these blocks.

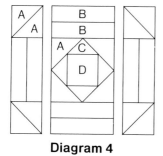

Diagram 4

8. Repeat Steps 1 through 7 to make the four IB blocks, changing the fabric in the center A triangles and in the B units, as shown in **Diagram 1.**

Block II

Refer to the **Fabric Key** and **Diagram 5** for fabric placement. Construct the blocks as follows, pressing the seams toward the darker fabrics. The fabric colors given in the directions are for the IIA Blocks. Make eight of these blocks first, then follow the same sequence to make nine of Block IIB, changing the fabrics as shown in **Diagram 5.**

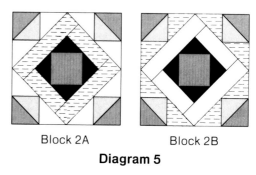

Block 2A Block 2B

Diagram 5

1. Sew a pastel blue C triangle to each side of a D square.

2. Add a light blue E rectangle to two opposite sides of the CD unit, and sew a light blue F rectangle to each of the other two opposite sides, as shown in **Diagram 6.**

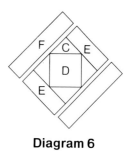

Diagram 6

3. To make the corner units, join a dark blue A triangle to a medium blue A triangle to form a square. Add a rose A triangle to each side of the medium blue triangle, as shown in **Diagram 7.** Make four of these corner units, and join them to the four sides of the center unit, as shown in **Diagram 8.** Make a total of eight of these blocks.

Diagram 7

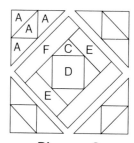

Diagram 8

4. Repeat Steps 1 through 3 to make nine IIB blocks, changing the fabric in the E and F pieces and in the A triangles, as shown in **Diagram 5.**

Assembling the Quilt Top

1. Referring to the **Quilt Diagram,** join the four kinds of blocks in seven horizontal rows in the order shown. Press the seams in opposite directions from row to row. Refer to page 159 for instructions on assembling quilt tops.

2. Join the rows, aligning the alternately pressed seams. The inner quilt top should measure 60½ × 84½ inches, including seam allowances.

3. Sew together the border strips before adding them to the quilt. Join the strips in the following order: light blue, 1½-inch-wide rose, medium blue, and 6½-inch-wide rose. Press the seams toward the outer borders.

4. Sew the borders to the quilt, mitering the border corners. Refer to page 159 for instructions on adding and mitering borders.

Quilting and Finishing

1. Layer the backing, batting, and quilt top; baste.

2. Quilt as desired. The blocks of the quilt shown were outline quilted ¼ inch from the seam lines.

3. Make French-fold binding from the remaining rose fabric. You will need approximately 396 inches (11 yards) of binding. Refer to page 164 for instructions on making and attaching binding. Sew the binding to the quilt, mitering the corners.

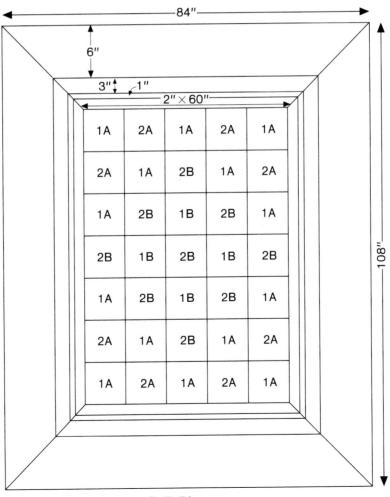

Quilt Diagram

Infinity

There's a lot going on in this stunning wallhanging. Three block patterns and eleven different fabrics could be chaotic; instead, there is an underlying sense of unity created by the same core group of fabrics appearing in all of the blocks. Play with different fabric and color placements, and establish a core fabric group. When you use these fabrics effectively, your blocks will appear to flow into each other.

Skill Level: Intermediate

Size: Finished quilt is 40 inches square
Finished blocks are 9 inches square

Fabrics and Supplies

Because of the individualized use of fabrics in this quilt, only general yardages are given, except for the borders. For each border, you will need at least the amount listed; purchase additional fabric if you intend to use it in the blocks as well. Eleven different fabrics were used in the quilt shown; you may choose to use more or fewer depending on your color and placement plan.

- ½ yard or more of Fabric 1 for blocks and outer border (teal in the quilt shown)
- ½ yard or more of Fabric 2 for blocks and middle border (blue print in quilt shown)
- ¼ yard or more *each* of Fabrics 3 and 4 for the pieced inner border (light blue and rose print in quilt shown)
- ¼ yard *each* or scraps of several assorted print and solid fabrics that coordinate with the border fabrics. Choose an assortment of fabrics in light, medium, and dark values for

good contrast. You will need a total of approximately 1¾ yards of fabric.

- 1¼ yards of fabric for the quilt back
- Quilt batting, larger than 40 inches square
- Rotary cutter, ruler, and mat
- Template plastic
- Colored pencils or crayons

Planning Your Quilt

The quilt is made up of three different block patterns: a Swing in the Center block in the center of the quilt, Rippling Star blocks on the sides, and Memory blocks in the corners. To try different color and fabric placement options for the blocks, make several photocopies of the **Quilt Diagram.** Using colored pencils or crayons, color the blocks in a manner that emphasizes certain shapes within the blocks and that you find pleasing. Work to create an interesting overall design. Coloring all four Rippling Star blocks and all four Memory blocks consistently will make piecing your quilt easier. Try to repeat some of the same colors and fabrics in all of the blocks to help break down the visual divisions between the individual blocks.

When you have created a color arrangement you like, select fabrics for your project. Your quilt

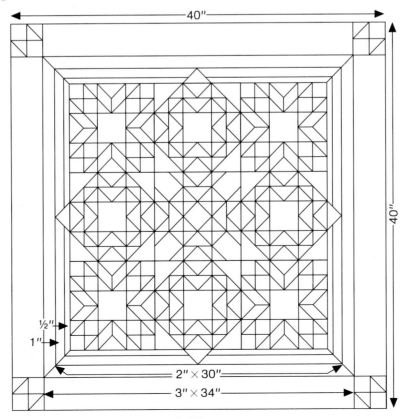

Quilt Diagram

will have richer visual texture if you use fabrics that are variations of essentially the same color in the areas that you have designated to be a particular color. For example, three *different* light-colored fabrics were used for the light areas in the quilt shown.

Refer to your colored diagram to cut the appropriate fabric pieces for each block.

Cutting

All patterns and measurements include ¼-inch seam allowances. Cut the largest fabric pieces first, then cut the smaller pieces from the remaining fabric.

The cutting instructions that follow give directions for quick-cutting with a rotary cutter all of the fabric pieces except E and H. Prepare plastic templates for patterns E and H (patterns appear on page 13). Instructions for making and using templates are on page 152. Note that for some of the pieces, the quick-cutting method will result in leftover strips of fabric.

If you prefer to cut all the pieces in a traditional manner, make templates for the following pieces (measurements include ¼-inch seam allowances):

- **A:** 3½-inch square
- **B:** 2-inch square
- **C:** Make a 2⅜-inch square; cut the square in half diagonally.
- **D:** Make a 4¼-inch square; cut the square in half diagonally both ways.
- **F:** 3⅞-inch square
- **G:** 2⅝-inch square

From Fabric 1, cut:
- Four 3½ × 44-inch outer border strips

From Fabric 2, cut:
- Four 2½ × 44-inch middle border strips

From Fabric 3, cut:
- Four 1½ × 44-inch inner border strips

From Fabric 4, cut:
- Four 1 × 44-inch inner border strips

For the Swing in the Center block,
using the fabrics you have chosen, cut:
- 32 C triangles

  Quick-Cutting Method: Cut a 2⅜ × 44-inch strip. Cut the strip into 2⅜-inch squares. You will need 16 squares. Cut each square in half diagonally to make two triangles.
- 8 D triangles

  Quick-Cutting Method: Cut a 4¼ × 44-inch strip. From the strip, cut two 4¼-inch squares. Cut each square in half diagonally in both directions to make four triangles.
- 1 G square

  Quick-Cutting Method: Cut one 2⅝-inch square.
- 4 H pieces

For the Memory blocks,
using the fabrics you have chosen, cut:
- 4 A squares

  Quick-Cutting Method: Cut a 3½ × 44-inch strip. From the strip, cut four 3½-inch squares.
- 32 B squares

  Quick-Cutting Method: Cut two 2 × 44-inch strips. Cut the strips into 2-inch squares.
- 96 C triangles

  Quick-Cutting Method: Cut three 2⅜ × 44-inch strips. Cut the strips into 2⅜-inch squares. You will need 48 squares. Cut each square in half diagonally to make two triangles.
- 16 D triangles

  Quick-Cutting Method: Cut a 4¼ × 44-inch strip. From the strip, cut four 4¼-inch squares. Cut each square in half diagonally in both directions to make four triangles.
- 16 E pieces and 16 E reverse pieces (Mark the E pieces with the right side of the template facing you. Turn the template over so the wrong side is facing you to mark the E reverse pieces.)

For the Rippling Star blocks,
using the fabrics you have chosen, cut:
- 4 A squares

  Quick-Cutting Method: Cut a 3½ × 44-inch strip. From the strip, cut four 3½-inch squares.
- 128 C triangles

  Quick-Cutting Method: Cut four 2⅜ × 44-inch strips. Cut the strips into 2⅜-inch squares. You will need 64 squares. Cut each square in half diagonally to make two triangles.
- 32 D triangles

  Quick-Cutting Method: Cut a 4¼ × 44-inch strip. From the strip, cut eight 4¼-inch squares. Cut each square in half diagonally in both directions to make four triangles.

- 16 F triangles

  Quick-Cutting Method: Cut a 3⅞ × 44-inch strip. From the strip, cut eight 3⅞-inch squares. Cut each square in half diagonally to make two triangles.

For the pieced inner border, using fabric that matches the outer D triangles on the Rippling Star blocks, cut:

- 4 D triangles

  Quick-Cutting Method: Cut one 4¼-inch square. Cut the square in half diagonally in both directions to make four triangles.

For the corner squares, using the fabrics you have chosen, cut:

- 8 B squares

  Quick-Cutting Method: Cut a 2 × 44-inch strip. From the strip, cut eight 2-inch squares.

- 16 C triangles

  Quick-Cutting Method: Cut a 2⅜ × 44-inch strip. From the strip, cut eight 2⅜-inch squares. Cut each square in half diagonally to make two triangles.

Piecing the Blocks

Referring to the block diagrams, lay out the block pieces according to your colored quilt plan. This will help keep things organized when piecing the blocks, since many of the same shapes are used in the different blocks.

Swing in the Center Block

1. Sew C triangles to three sides of an H piece, as shown in **Diagram 1.** Make a total of four of these units. Press the seams away from the H piece.

Diagram 1

2. Sew a C triangle to each short side of a D triangle. Press the seams away from the D triangle. Make eight of these units. Sew together the CD units in pairs, positioning them as shown in **Diagram 2.** You should have four pairs.

Diagram 2

3. Sew a C triangle to each side of a G square to make the center of the block. Press the seam allowances away from the G square.

4. Referring to the **Swing in the Center Piecing Diagram,** sew the units into horizontal rows, making sure they are positioned correctly. Press the seam allowances in opposite directions from row to row.

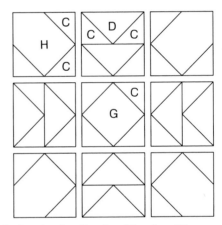

Swing in the Center Piecing Diagram

5. Join the three rows, as shown in the **Swing in the Center Block Diagram.** Press the seam allowances in one direction. You will need only one Swing in the Center block.

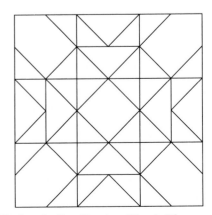

Swing in the Center Block Diagram

Memory Blocks

1. Sew together two C triangles to make a square. Repeat to make a second square. Join these to two B squares, pressing the seam toward the B squares. Join the two units to make a four-patch, as shown in **Diagram 3.** Make four of these units.

Diagram 3

2. Join a C triangle to an E piece, as shown in **Diagram 4.** In the same manner, join a C triangle to an E reverse piece. Sew together these two units, as shown. Set a D triangle into the open side. Instructions for setting-in pieces are on page 155. Make four of these units.

Diagram 4

3. Using an A square as the center of the middle row, join the units together in horizontal rows, making sure the pieces are positioned as shown in the **Memory Piecing Diagram.** Press the seam allowances in opposite directions from row to row.

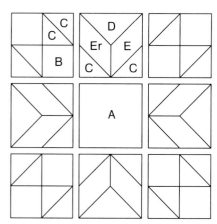

Memory Piecing Diagram

4. Join the rows together, as shown in the **Memory Block Diagram.** Press the seam allowances in one direction. Make a total of four Memory blocks.

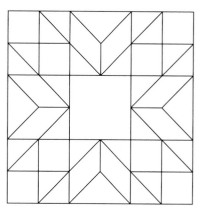

Memory Block Diagram

Rippling Star Blocks

1. Join two C triangles along the long sides to form a square. Sew C triangles to two sides of the square to form a larger triangle, as shown in **Diagram 5.** Sew an F triangle to the long side of the pieced triangle, as shown in **Diagram 5.** Make four of these units.

Diagram 5

2. Sew a C triangle to each short side of a D triangle. Make eight of these units. Press the seams away from the D triangle. Join the CD units together in pairs, positioning them as shown in **Diagram 6.** You should have four pairs.

Diagram 6

3. Using an A square as the center of the middle row, sew the units into horizontal rows, making sure the pieces are positioned as shown in the **Rippling Star Piecing Diagram.** Press the seams in opposite directions from row to row.

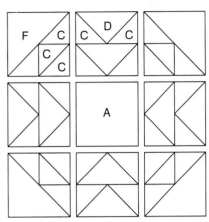

Rippling Star Piecing Diagram

4. Join the rows together, as shown in the **Rippling Star Block Diagram.** Press the seams in one direction. Make a total of four Rippling Star blocks.

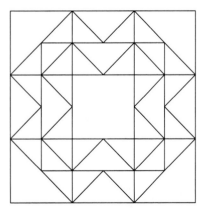

Rippling Star Block Diagram

Piecing the Inner Border

1. Join a 1½-inch-wide Fabric 3 border strip to a 1-inch-wide Fabric 4 border strip along the long sides. Press the seams away from the 1-inch border. Repeat to make a total of four pieced borders.

2. Cut each pieced border into two pieces, each approximately 20 inches long. Using a rotary cutter and ruler or triangle template as a guide, trim one end of each border at a 45 degree angle, as shown in **Diagram 7.** The two border sections must be trimmed with angles in opposite directions so a D triangle piece will fit between them.

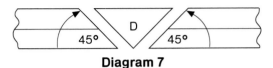

Diagram 7

3. To complete one inner border, sew the angled ends of the border sections to the sides of a D triangle, as shown in **Diagram 7.** The D triangles should match the outside triangles on the Rippling Star blocks. (Refer to the **Quilt Diagram** for reference on how these should match.) Make four of these inner pieced borders.

Piecing the Outer Border Corner Squares

1. Join two C triangles to make a square. Make two of these squares. Referring to **Diagram 8,** join the pieced squares to B squares, pressing the seams toward the B squares. Join the two units to make four border corner squares.

Diagram 8

Assembling the Quilt Top

1. Referring to your colored quilt plan, sew together the nine blocks in three rows with three blocks in each row. Press the seam allowances in opposite directions from row to row. Join the rows. Refer to page 159 for instructions on assembling quilt tops.

2. Center and sew an inner pieced border to one long side of each 2½-inch-wide Fabric 2 middle border strip. Press the seam allowances toward the middle border.

3. Center and sew the joined inner and middle border units to each side of the quilt top, placing the inner borders along the edges of the quilt top. Make sure the D triangles align with the outer triangles in the Rippling Star blocks. Press the seam allowances toward the borders. Miter the corner seams, mitering all the borders in one step. See page 159 for instructions on adding and mitering borders.

4. Measure the quilt top and trim the outer border strips to this length. Sew borders to two opposite sides of the quilt top.

5. Sew pieced border corner squares to opposite ends of the remaining two outer border strips. Sew the borders to the remaining sides of the quilt top.

Quilting and Finishing

1. Select and mark quilting designs on the quilt top.

2. Layer the backing, batting, and quilt top; baste.

3. Quilt all marked designs.

4. Bind the quilt with spiral-pieced bias binding. To make this type of binding, cut an assortment of fabric strips, ranging from 1½ to 4 inches wide, from the remaining fabric scraps.

5. Join the strips along the long sides in random order, staggering the strips to create an angled end, as shown in **Diagram 9**. Press all the seam allowances in the same direction.

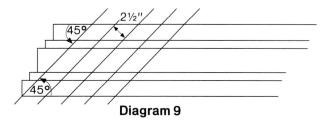

Diagram 9

6. Trim one end of the strip at a 45 degree angle. Referring to **Diagram 9**, cut 2½-inch-wide bias strips parallel to the trimmed edge. Sew the strips together end to end to make a strip approximately 170 inches long. Make more bias strips as needed to reach this length.

7. Stitch the spiral binding around the perimeter of the quilt, mitering the corners. Refer to page 164 for instructions on making and attaching binding.

8. Turn under ¼ inch on the binding. Bring the folded edge around to the quilt back and blindstitch in place. See page 167 for instructions for making and attaching a hanging sleeve.

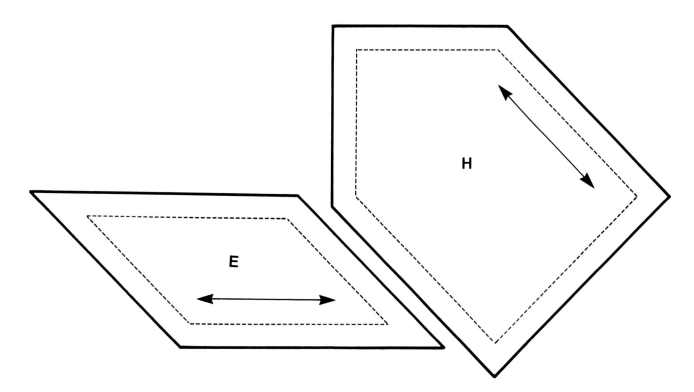

Amish Nine Patch

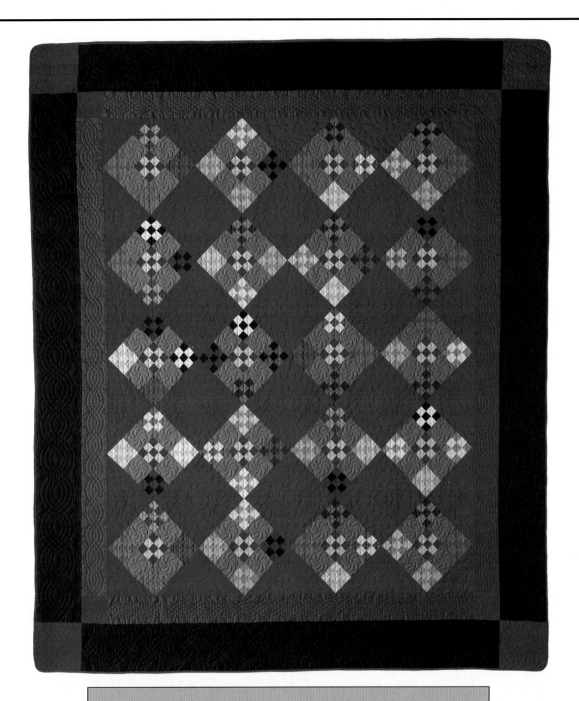

The sparkling colors in this quilt leave no doubt that it follows the Amish tradition. Although some of the colors stray from "classic" Amish, the design itself, with double Nine-Patch blocks, wide borders, and corner squares, is very typical of antique Amish quilts. Quick-cutting and strip-piecing techniques let you zip through all the Nine-Patch blocks. Setting squares and wide borders leave lots of room for quilting.

Skill Level: Easy

Size: Finished quilt is 88½ × 104⅜ inches
Finished block is 11¼ inches square

Fabrics and Supplies

- 3½ yards of solid fuchsia fabric for setting squares, setting triangles, border squares, and binding
- 3 yards of solid black fabric for outer borders and patchwork
- 2½ yards of solid purple fabric for inner borders and patchwork
- 1½ yards of solid royal blue fabric for patchwork
- ¼ yard *each,* or scraps, of approximately 40 solid-color fabrics for patchwork. (You will need at least three 1⅞ × 9-inch strips from each fabric.)
- 8 yards of fabric for quilt backing
- King-size quilt batting (120 inches square)
- Rotary cutter, ruler, and mat

Cutting

All measurements include a ¼-inch seam allowance. Measurements for the borders are longer than needed; trim them to the exact length when they are added to the quilt top. Instructions given are for quick-cutting the pieces with a rotary cutter and ruler.

From the solid fuchsia fabric, cut:
- Twelve 11¾-inch setting squares
- 14 side setting triangles

  Quick-Cutting Method: Cut four 17⅛-inch squares. Cut each square in half diagonally in both directions to make four triangles. You will have two extra triangles.
- 4 corner setting triangles

  Quick-Cutting Method: Cut two 8⅞-inch squares. Cut each square in half diagonally to make two triangles.
- Four 5-inch inner border corner squares
- Four 8½-inch outer border corner squares

From the solid black fabric, cut:
- Two 8½ × 95-inch side border strips and two 8½ × 79-inch top and bottom border strips

- Save the remaining fabric for small Nine-Patch blocks

From the solid purple fabric, cut:
- Two 5 × 90-inch side border strips and two 5 × 70-inch top and bottom border strips
- Save the remaining fabric for small Nine-Patch blocks

From the solid royal blue fabric, cut:
- Eighty 4¼-inch squares

  Quick-Cutting Method: Cut nine 4¼ × 44-inch strips. Cut these strips into 4¼-inch squares.
- Save the remaining fabric for small Nine-Patch blocks

From the ¼-yard pieces (or scraps) of solid-color fabrics, cut:
- 1¾ × 9-inch strips. (You will need a total of 300 strips. Start by cutting three strips from each fabric. Cut additional strips as needed, using your favorite color combinations.)

Piecing the Blocks

1. Sort the short fabric strips into pairs of colors for the small Nine Patches. For best results, create pairs that have a high degree of contrast. In the **Fabric Key** and the diagrams, Color One is shown as a dark color, and Color Two is shown as a light color.

Fabric Key

Color 1

Color 2

2. For each pair, make two types of strip sets with three strips in each set, as shown in **Diagram 1.** Use two strips of Color One and one strip of Color Two for Strip Set A. Use the opposite arrangement of the colors for Strip Set B. Join the strips with ¼-inch seams. Press the seams toward the darker fabric strips.

3. Cut the strip sets into 1¾-inch-wide A and B strip sequences, as shown in **Diagram 1.** You should be able to cut five strip sequences from each strip set.

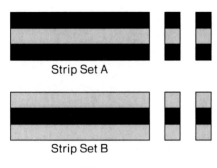

Strip Set A

Strip Set B

Diagram 1

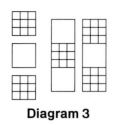

Diagram 3

4. Use A and B strip sequences to make the small Nine-Patch blocks. You can arrange the blocks in two different combinations, as shown in **Diagram 2.** The pressed seams should lie in opposite directions when you join the rows. The blocks should measure 4¼ inches, including seam allowances.

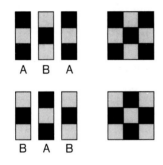

A   B   A

B   A   B

Diagram 2

5. In this manner, make 100 small Nine-Patch blocks, cutting more 1¾ × 9-inch strips as needed. The quilt shown has as many as 20 and as few as 1 of some of the color combinations. Each time you cut three strips each from two different colors and make them into A and B Strip Sets, you will be able to make three blocks, two of one type and one of the other. The quilt shown uses the same color combination Nine Patches in the center position of all the Double Nine-Patch blocks.

6. For each of the 20 Double Nine-Patch blocks needed for the quilt, combine five small Nine-Patch blocks and four 4¼-inch blue squares.

Join the blocks and squares in rows, as shown in **Diagram 3.** Press the seams toward the blue squares. Join the rows, aligning the seams. The pressed seam allowances should face in opposite directions. The blocks should measure 11¾ inches square, including seam allowances.

Assembling the Quilt Top

1. Lay out the Double Nine-Patch blocks, setting squares, side setting triangles, and corner setting triangles, as shown in the **Quilt Diagram.**

2. Join the blocks and setting pieces in diagonal rows, pressing the seams in opposite directions from row to row. Join the rows, aligning the seams. The pressed seam allowances should face in opposite directions. Refer to page 159 for instructions on assembling quilt tops. The completed quilt top before the borders are added should measure 64 × 79⅞ inches, including seam allowances.

3. Measure the long sides of the quilt top. Trim the two 5 × 90-inch purple border strips to this length. Sew one border strip to each side of the quilt top. Press the seam toward the border. Measure the width of your quilt top. Trim the two 5 × 70-inch purple border strips to this length. Sew a 5-inch fuchsia corner square to each end of these strips. Press the seams toward the border strips. Sew the two border strips to the two opposite ends of the quilt top. Press the seams toward the borders.

4. In the same manner, trim and sew the 8½ × 95-inch black border strips to the quilt sides. Measure and trim the 8½ × 79-inch black border strips, and add an 8½-inch fuchsia corner square to each end. Sew the two border strips to the opposite ends of the quilt top, and press the seams toward the borders. The completed quilt top should measure 89 × 104⅞ inches, including seam allowances.

Quilting and Finishing

1. Mark quilting designs as desired. The quilt shown has a daisy design in the blue squares, feather circles in the fuchsia squares, and cables in the borders. It also has diagonal lines quilted from corner to corner both ways in each square of the small Nine Patches.

2. Divide the quilt backing fabric into three 96-inch (2⅔-yard) lengths. Piece the three lengths to make a quilt back with seams running parallel to the short sides of the quilt. Press the seam open.

3. Layer the quilt back, batting, and quilt top; baste. Quilt all marked designs.

4. Make French-fold binding from the remaining fuchsia fabric. You will need approximately 395 inches (10¾ yards) of binding for the quilt. See page 164 for instructions on making and attaching binding. Sew the binding to the quilt. The quilt shown has gently rounded, rather than mitered, corners.

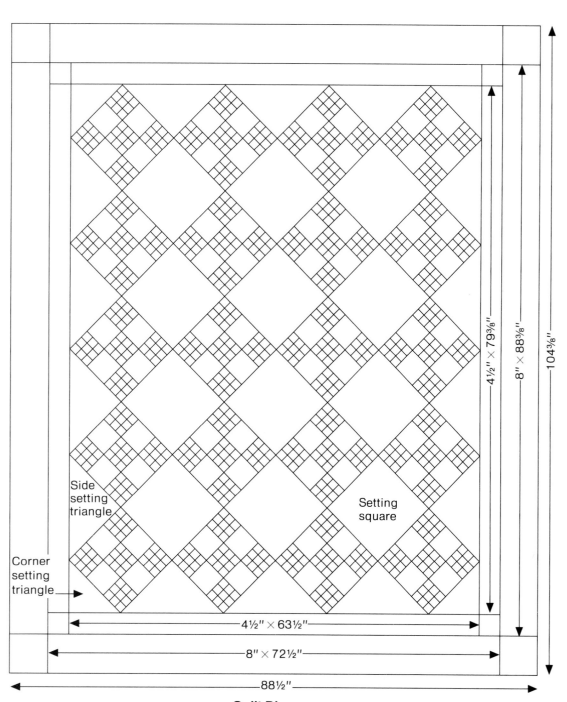

Quilt Diagram

Yankee Barter

It's hard to take your eyes off the feathered star, appliquéd vines and ribbons, and elaborate trapunto at the center of this medallion quilt. An elegant design and exquisite workmanship make this quilt a real showpiece. If you love the challenge of intricate piecing, delicate appliqué, and trapunto, here is a quilt to show off all your skills.

Skill Level: Challenging

Size: Finished quilt is approximately 79 × 86 inches

Fabrics and Supplies

- 5½ yards of muslin for patchwork and borders
- 3 yards of solid light blue fabric for patchwork and borders
- 3 yards of blue-and-pink floral stripe fabric for borders
- 1 yard of black print fabric for appliqué pieces and borders
- ½ yard of solid rose fabric for patchwork and appliqué pieces
- ⅓ yard dark navy print fabric for patchwork
- ¼ yard of light blue print fabric for appliqué pieces
- 6 yards of fabric for the quilt back
- Queen-size quilt batting (90 × 108 inches)
- Rotary cutter, ruler, and mat
- Template plastic
- Tracing paper
- Black permanent felt-tip pen
- Thread to match the appliqué fabrics
- White acrylic yarn and blunt needle for trapunto (optional)

Cutting

All patchwork template patterns and measurements include ¼-inch seam allowances. Quick-cutting instructions are given for many of the patchwork shapes; note that for some of the pieces, the quick-cutting method may result in leftover strips of fabric. For the other shapes, prepare plastic templates using the patterns on pages 23 and 26. Instructions for making and using templates are on page 152. To mark reverse pieces, turn the templates over so the wrong side is facing up. If you prefer to cut all the pieces in a traditional manner, make additional templates for the following pieces (measurements include ¼-inch seam allowances):

- **A:** Make a 2⅜-inch square; cut the square in half diagonally.
- **B:** 2-inch square
- **F:** 10⅛-inch square

Prepare templates for the appliqué shapes using the **Corner Appliqué Pattern** and the **Ribbon and Vine Appliqué Patterns** on pages 24 and 25. These pieces do not include seam allowances; add seam allowances to the fabric pieces when cutting them.

From the muslin, cut:

- Two 10 × 93-inch side border strips
- Two 14 × 93-inch top and bottom border strips
- Four 5½ × 60-inch border strips
- 8 F squares
- One 10-inch center square
- 80 A triangles

  Quick-Cutting Method: Cut eight 2⅜-inch strips across the width of the fabric (approximately 14 inches after the border strips have been cut). From the strips, cut forty 2⅜-inch squares; cut each square in half diagonally to make two triangles.

From the solid light blue fabric, cut:

- Four 1½ × 100-inch border strips
- Four 1½ × 60-inch border strips
- Sixteen 1½ × 13-inch strips
- 8 B squares

  Quick-Cutting Method: Cut a 2-inch strip across the width of the fabric (approximately 30 inches after the border strips have been cut). From this strip, cut eight 2-inch squares.

- 8 C diamonds
- 64 A triangles

  Quick-Cutting Method: Cut three 2⅜-inch strips across the width of the fabric. From the strips, cut thirty-two 2⅜-inch squares; cut each square in half diagonally to make two triangles.

From the blue-and-pink floral stripe fabric, cut:

- Four 3¾ × 100-inch border strips
- Four 3¾ × 60-inch border strips
- Four 1½ × 13-inch strips

From the black print fabric, cut:

- Sixteen 1 × 44-inch border strips. Join the strips together with diagonal bias seams into one long strip. From this long strip, cut four 60-inch-long border strips and four 100-inch-long border strips.

- 8 approximately ¾ × 20-inch bias pieces
- 40 leaves

From the solid rose fabric, cut:
- 4 D triangles
- 4 Ribbon B pieces and 4 Ribbon B reverse pieces
- 4 Ribbon D pieces and 4 Ribbon D reverse pieces
- 8 approximately ¾ × 6-inch bias pieces

From the dark navy print fabric, cut:
- 8 E pieces

From the light blue print fabric, cut:
- 4 Corner A appliqué pieces
- 4 Corner B pieces and 4 Corner B reverse pieces
- 4 Corner C pieces
- 4 Ribbon A pieces and 4 Ribbon A reverse pieces
- 4 Ribbon C pieces and 4 Ribbon C reverse pieces

Piecing the Feathered Star

1. To piece the center of the star, sew a 1½ × 13-inch floral stripe fabric strip to each side of the center muslin square, mitering the corners. For tips on mitering, see page 159. Press seam allowances toward the strips. The center square should measure 11 inches, including seam allowances.

2. Join pairs of solid light blue and muslin A triangles along the long sides into squares. Press the seam allowances toward the blue fabric. Make 64 pieced squares.

3. Join four of the pieced squares together into a strip, with the triangles positioned as shown in **Diagram 1**. Add a muslin A triangle to one end of the strip and a solid light blue B square to the other end. Press the seam allowances toward the blue pieces. Make eight of these units.

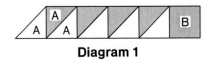

Diagram 1

4. Join four of the pieced squares into a strip with the triangles positioned as shown in **Diagram 2**. Add a muslin A triangle to one end of the strip. Press the seam allowances toward the blue pieces. Make eight of these units.

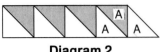

Diagram 2

5. Refer to **Diagram 3** to make the points of the star. First, sew a rose D triangle onto one short side of a navy E piece, forming a DE triangle. Press the seam allowances toward the navy piece. Then, sew a unit from Step 3 onto one side of a second navy E piece, as shown, pressing the seam allowance toward the E piece. Sew a unit from Step 4 onto one side of the B square. Join this section to the DE triangle, pressing the seam allowances toward the triangle. Make a total of four of these units.

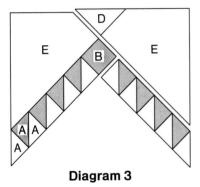

Diagram 3

6. To make the Center Section, sew a Step 5 unit to two opposite sides of the center square, as shown in **Diagram 4**. Press the seams in one direction. Set this section aside for now.

7. Sew 1½ × 13-inch solid light blue strips to two adjacent sides of each of the eight muslin F squares. Miter the corner seam. Press the seams toward the strips. Leave the excess strips hanging at the sides of the squares.

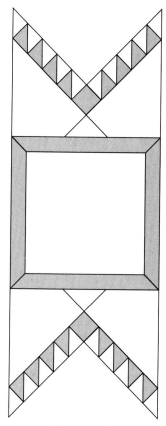

Diagram 4

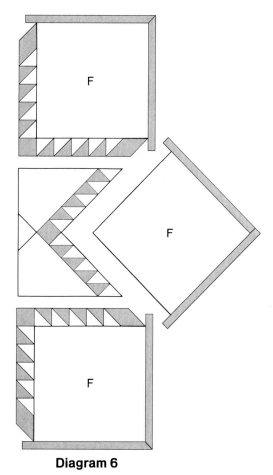

unsewn and untrimmed. See page 155 for tips on setting-in pieces. Repeat to make a second identical Side Section.

Diagram 6

8. Referring to **Diagram 5,** sew a solid light blue C diamond to one end of a Step 3 unit. Sew a solid light blue C diamond to one end of a Step 4 unit, as shown. Sew the Step 3 unit and the Step 4 unit to two adjacent sides of a muslin F square. Check to make sure the triangles are positioned as shown. Press the seams away from the muslin square. Make four of these units. You should have four muslin F squares left over.

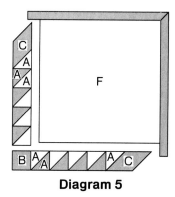

Diagram 5

9. To make a Side Section, sew a Step 8 unit to two opposite sides of a Step 5 unit, as shown in **Diagram 6.** Set one of the muslin squares into the triangular opening, leaving the solid light blue strips

10. Referring to **Diagram 7,** sew the two Side Sections to opposite sides of the Center Section. Set a muslin F square into each triangular opening, leaving the solid light blue strips unsewn and untrimmed.

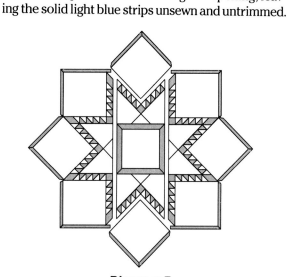

Diagram 7

Piecing and Adding the Inner Border Unit

1. Sew together 60-inch border strips in the following order: muslin, solid light blue, floral stripe, and black print. Press all the seam allowances away from the muslin border. Make four of these inner border units.

2. Stitch together and trim the ends of the solid light blue strips before adding the borders. To finish these strips, lay the end of one strip out flat. Turn under the end of the adjacent strip so that it forms a mitered angle, and appliqué it in place on top of the first strip. Trim away the excess strips on the back side of the quilt.

3. Referring to the **Quilt Diagram,** pin the border units to the solid light blue strips on the sides of the star. The border will go under the points of the F squares on the sides, as indicated by the dashed lines on the diagram. Fold the points out of the way while you are stitching on the borders. Stitch the borders to the star, stopping the stitching where the points begin and resuming it on the other side. Miter the border corner seams. For tips on adding and mitering borders, see page 159.

4. After the borders have been stitched on, unfold the points of the F squares into position on top of the borders and pin them into place. Appliqué the light blue edges of the squares to the borders where they overlap. Trim the borders from behind the squares.

Appliquéing the Ribbon Designs

1. The **Ribbon and Vine Appliqué Pattern** is given in two parts on page 25. Trace the two parts and join them on the line where indicated to make the whole pattern. Using a permanent pen, darken the lines on the tracing paper pattern. Use this pattern as a master pattern to guide the placement of the appliqué pieces. Make a similar pattern for the **Corner Appliqué Pattern** on page 24.

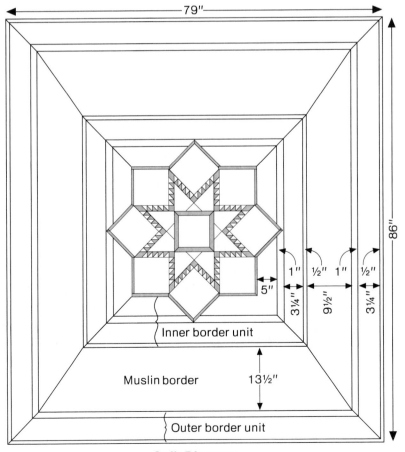

Quilt Diagram

2. Using the ¾-inch-wide bias strips, prepare ⅛-inch-wide bias pieces. See page 157 for instructions on making bias strips.

3. Using a pencil or other removable marker, draw positioning guidelines for the appliqué designs onto the muslin borders at each corner. Pin or baste the appliqué pieces within the positioning guidelines. Using matching thread colors, appliqué the pieces in place.

Adding the Remaining Borders

1. Sew 10-inch-wide muslin border strips to the two sides of the quilt top. Sew 14-inch-wide muslin border strips to the top and bottom. Miter the border corner seams. Press the seams away from the quilt center.

2. To make an outer border unit, sew together 100-inch-long border strips in the following order: solid light blue, floral stripe, and black print. Press the seams away from the light blue strip.

3. Sew an outer border unit to each side of the quilt top. Sew the remaining two border units to the top and bottom. Miter the border corner seams. Press the seam allowances away from the quilt center.

Quilting and Finishing

1. Mark quilting designs of your choice on the quilt top. The quilt shown is quilted with feathered circle designs in the muslin squares and flowing feather designs in the wide muslin borders. Echo quilting around the appliqué pieces and a diagonal grid complete the design. See page 160 for tips on echo quilting.

2. To piece the quilt back, divide the yardage into two 3-yard pieces. Divide one of those pieces in half lengthwise, and sew each half to a long side of the other 3-yard piece. Layer the quilt back, batting, and quilt top; baste.

3. Quilt all marked designs. If you wish, enhance the fancy quilting with stuffed quilting, or *trapunto*. Instructions for trapunto can be found in "Adding Trapunto for Extra Elegance" on page 24.

4. When quilting is complete, trim the quilt back and batting even with the quilt top. Trim away an extra ¼ inch of batting. Turn in ¼ inch on the quilt top and quilt back. Blindstitch the folded edges together around the perimeter of the quilt.

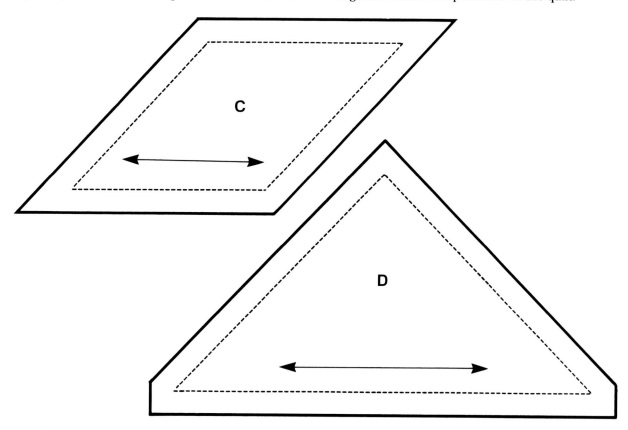

ADDING TRAPUNTO FOR EXTRA ELEGANCE

The beauty of this quilt is enhanced by extra filler, or *trapunto,* in the feathered circle quilting designs. Trapunto was also used to great effect in Here's My Heart (page 27), Lilies of the Field (page 107), and Carnation Carousel (page 139). It's an extra-special touch that can really make a quilt stand out. The stuffing is done after the quilt is quilted and the edges are bound. Follow the instructions below to add trapunto to your quilt.

You will need a 6-inch-long blunt-point trapunto needle and white 100 percent acrylic yarn, such as the type used for package ties.

1. Cut a 15-inch length of yarn. If your yarn is three-ply, separate it and use only one ply at a time. Thread the needle with a single strand of yarn.

2. Turn the quilt over to the back. Choose an area to be stuffed and insert the needle between the fabric threads by gently rubbing the blunt point against the threads. Run the needle between the layers of the quilt, across the area to be stuffed, and bring the point out.

3. Pull the yarn gently into the area to be filled. Clip the end of the yarn close to the quilt back. If necessary, use your needle to poke the end of yarn back into the quilt. Continue to add lengths of yarn until the area is puffy but not tight. When stuffing large channels, overlap the ends of the yarn by about ½ inch to help fill the areas uniformly.

4. Smooth over large needle holes with your fingernail. Fabric is fairly flexible, and the holes will largely disappear after the quilt is washed one time. ◆

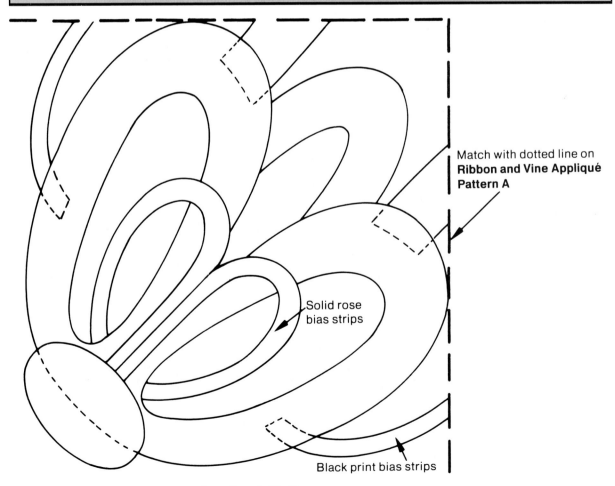

Match with dotted line on
**Ribbon and Vine Appliqué
Pattern A**

Solid rose
bias strips

Black print bias strips

Corner Appliqué Pattern

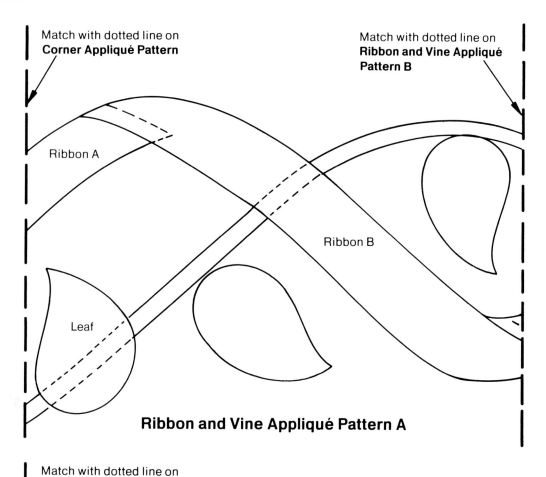

Match with dotted line on
Corner Appliqué Pattern

Match with dotted line on
Ribbon and Vine Appliqué Pattern B

Ribbon A

Ribbon B

Leaf

Ribbon and Vine Appliqué Pattern A

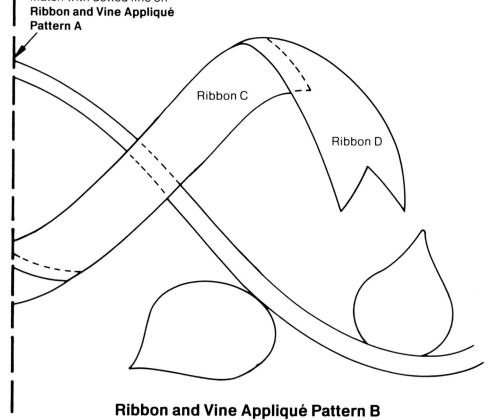

Match with dotted line on
Ribbon and Vine Appliqué Pattern A

Ribbon C

Ribbon D

Ribbon and Vine Appliqué Pattern B

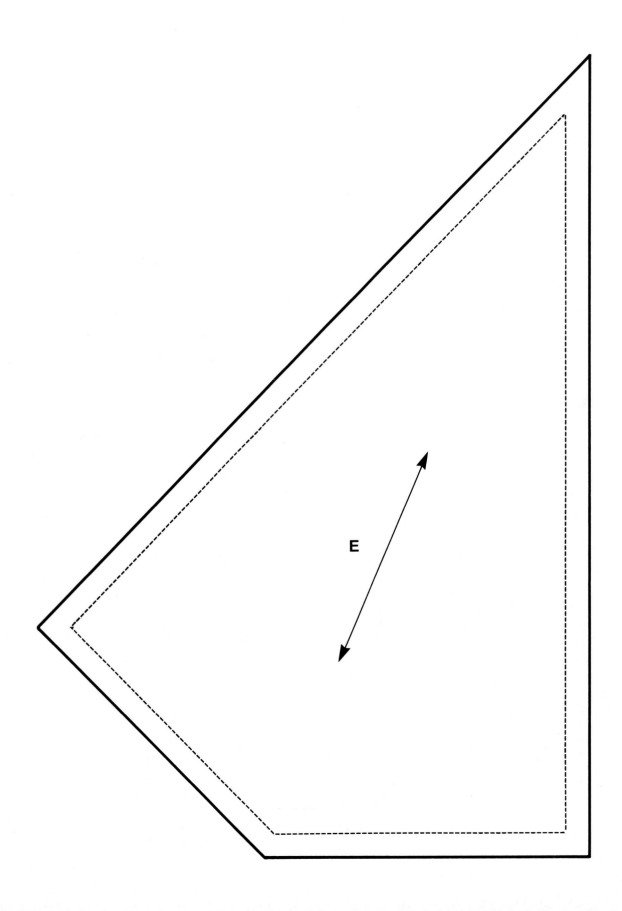

Here's My Heart

The traditional Irish Chain pattern gets a new twist in this pretty wallhanging with the addition of appliqué hearts. Quick-and-easy pieced blocks alternate with simple appliqué blocks. A delicate trapunto pattern surrounding the hearts adds an extra-special touch.

Skill Level: Easy

Size: Finished quilt is 63 inches square
Finished block is 10 inches square

Fabrics and Supplies

- 3 yards of blue print fabric for blocks, appliqués, and outer border
- 2½ yards of muslin for blocks, inner border, and binding
- ¾ yard of white print fabric for blocks
- 4 yards of muslin for quilt back
- Twin-size quilt batting (72 × 90 inches)
- Rotary cutter, ruler, and mat
- Template plastic
- Thread to match the appliqué fabrics
- White acrylic yarn and blunt needle for trapunto (optional)

Cutting

The instructions are written for quick-cutting and quick-piecing the pieced blocks using a rotary cutter and ruler. The measurements for all pieces include ¼-inch seam allowances. For the small square in the heart blocks, follow the quick-cutting directions or make a template (measurement includes ¼-inch seam allowance):

- **A:** 2½-inch square

Referring to the appliqué instructions on page 156, and using the **Heart Appliqué Pattern** on page 30, make a plastic template for the heart. Tips for making and using templates are on page 152. The pattern is the finished size; add seam allowances when cutting the pieces from the fabric.

From the blue print fabric, cut:
- Four 5½ × 67-inch outer border strips
- Twelve 2½ × 44-inch strips for the pieced blocks
- 12 hearts
- Forty-eight A squares for the heart blocks
  Quick-Cutting Method: Cut three 2½ × 44-inch strips; cut the strips into 2½-inch squares.

From the 2½-yard piece of muslin, cut:
- Four 2 × 54-inch inner border strips

- Four 2½ × 44-inch strips for the pieced blocks
- Twelve 10½-inch squares for the heart blocks
- Reserve the remaining fabric for binding

From the white print fabric, cut:
- Nine 2½ × 44-inch strips for the pieced blocks

Making the Pieced Blocks

Make 13 pieced blocks for the quilt. Follow the quick-piecing instructions below to make the rows, then assemble the rows into blocks.

Making Row A
1. Referring to the **Fabric Key** and **Diagram 1**, make a strip set by sewing together 2½-inch-wide strips in the following order: white, blue, muslin, blue, and white. Press the seam allowances toward the blue strips. Repeat to make a second identical strip set.

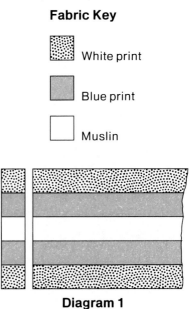

Fabric Key

White print

Blue print

Muslin

Diagram 1
Strip Set for Row A

2. Cut 2½-inch-wide segments from the strip set. Each segment is a Row A. Cut a total of 26 segments from the strip sets, two for each block, and set aside.

Making Row B

1. Referring to the **Fabric Key** and **Diagram 2,** make a strip set by sewing together 2½-inch-wide strips in the following order: blue, white, blue, white, and blue. Press the seam allowances toward the blue strips. Repeat to make a second identical strip set.

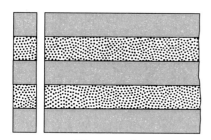

Diagram 2
Strip Set for Row B

2. Cut 2½-inch-wide segments from the strip set. Each segment is a Row B. Cut a total of 26 segments from the strip sets, two for each block, and set aside.

Making Row C

1. Referring to the **Fabric Key** and **Diagram 3,** make a strip set by sewing together 2½-inch-wide strips in the following order: muslin, blue, white, blue, and muslin. Press the seam allowances toward the blue strips.

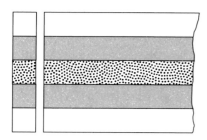

Diagram 3
Strip Set for Row C

2. Cut 2½-inch-wide segments from the strip set. Each segment is a Row C. Cut a total of 13 segments from the strip sets, one for each block.

Assembling the Block

1. Referring to **Diagram 4,** join the rows into a block by sewing them together in the following order:

Row A, Row B, Row C, Row B, and Row A. Repeat, making a total of 13 blocks.

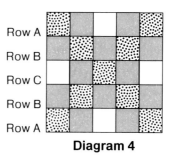

Row A
Row B
Row C
Row B
Row A

Diagram 4

Making the Heart Blocks

1. Appliqué a 2½-inch blue square in each corner of the twelve 10½-inch muslin squares, as shown in **Diagram 5.** See page 156 for tips on hand appliqué.

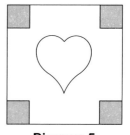

Diagram 5

2. Using a pencil or other removable marker, trace the **Heart Quilting Design** on page 31 onto the center of each of the muslin squares.

3. Appliqué a blue heart onto each square, using the center heart outline of the quilting design as a placement guideline.

Assembling the Quilt Top

1. Referring to the **Quilt Diagram,** sew together the pieced blocks and heart blocks in rows. Press the seams in alternate directions from row to row. Join the rows to complete the inner quilt. Refer to page 159 for instructions on assembling quilt tops. The quilt top should measure 50½ inches square, including seam allowances, before the borders are added.

2. Center a muslin border strip on each blue border strip and stitch the strips together. Press the seam allowances toward the blue strips.

3. Sew the borders to the quilt top, placing the muslin border next to the quilt and mitering the border corner seams. See page 159 for instructions on adding and mitering borders. Press the seam allowances away from the quilt center.

Quilting and Finishing

1. Mark quilting designs on the borders. The quilt shown has small hearts quilted in the muslin border and clamshells in the wide blue border. Draw a diagonal line from corner to corner each way through each small square, extending the lines into the background of the heart blocks.

2. Piece the quilt back with a vertical seam in the center, and trim so it is at least 3 inches larger than the quilt top on all sides. Layer the quilt back, batting, and top; baste.

3. Quilt all marked designs. If desired, add additional stuffing, called *trapunto,* in the feather shapes around the appliqué hearts. Instructions for trapunto are in "Adding Trapunto for Extra Elegance" on page 24.

4. From the remaining muslin, cut approximately 270 inches (7½ yards) of French-fold binding. See

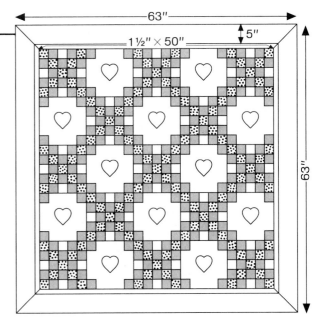

Quilt Diagram

page 164 for suggested binding widths and instructions on making and attaching bindings.

5. Sew the binding to the quilt top. Trim the excess batting and backing, and hand finish the binding on the wrong side of the quilt. If desired, sew a hanging sleeve to the quilt back. Instructions for adding a hanging sleeve are on page 167.

Heart Appliqué Pattern

Heart Quilting Design

Miniature Iowa Amish Star

Jewel-tone fabrics make this miniature quilt positively sparkle. The tiny star medallion is ringed by a series of pieced and simple borders to give you a quilt that is roughly the size of a single newspaper page. The black and bright solids give this quilt an Amish look, but it would be equally charming pieced from a variety of printed fabrics.

Skill Level: Easy

Size: Finished quilt is 17½ × 20½ inches
Finished center block is 4 inches square

Fabrics and Supplies

- ⅔ yard of solid black fabric for borders and quilt back
- ¼ yard of solid fuchsia fabric for center star and pieced border
- ¼ yard *each* of solid blue and solid teal fabrics for borders
- ⅛ yard or scraps of solid gray fabric for background of center star
- Lightweight quilt batting or cotton flannel, larger than 17½ × 20½ inches
- Template plastic
- Rotary cutter, ruler, and mat

Cutting

All template patterns and measurements include ¼-inch seam allowances. Instructions for making and using templates are on page 152. Quick-cutting instructions for rotary cutters are listed for the borders and the star block pieces. Note that for some of the pieces, the quick-cutting method will result in leftover strips of fabric. If you prefer to cut the block pieces in a traditional manner, make templates for the following pieces (measurements include ¼-inch seam allowances):

- **A:** 1½-inch square
- **B:** Make a 1⅞-inch square; cut the square in half diagonally.
- **C:** Make a 2⅜-inch square; cut the square in half diagonally.
- **D:** 2-inch square

From the solid black fabric, cut:
- One 21 × 24-inch rectangle for the quilt back
- Two 2 × 15-inch K borders
- 24 C triangles

  Quick-Cutting Method: Cut a 2⅜ × 44-inch strip. From the strip cut twelve 2⅜-inch squares; cut each square in half diagonally to make two triangles.

From the solid fuchsia fabric, cut:
- 24 C triangles

  Quick-Cutting Method: Cut a 2⅜ × 44-inch strip. From the strip, cut twelve 2⅜-inch squares; cut each square in half diagonally to make two triangles.

- 4 D squares

  Quick-Cutting Method: Cut a 2 × 44-inch strip. From the strip, cut four 2-inch squares.

- 12 B triangles

  Quick-Cutting Method: Cut a 1⅞ × 44-inch strip. From the strip, cut six 1⅞-inch squares; cut each square in half diagonally to make two triangles.

From the solid blue fabric, cut:
- Two 2 × 15-inch K borders and two 2 × 21-inch L borders

  Quick-Cutting Method: Cut two 2 × 44-inch strips. From each of the strips, cut a 15-inch-long K border and a 21-inch-long L border.

- Two 1½ × 4½-inch C borders and two 1½ × 6½-inch D borders

  Quick-Cutting Method: Cut a 1½ × 44-inch strip; all four borders can be cut from this one strip.

From the solid teal fabric, cut:
- Two 1¾ × 12½-inch I borders and two 1¾ × 15-inch J borders

  Quick-Cutting Method: Cut two 1¾ × 44-inch strips. From one strip, cut two 12½-inch-long I borders. From the second strip, cut two 15-inch-long J borders.

- Two 2 × 6½-inch E borders and two 2 × 9½-inch F borders

  Quick-Cutting Method: Cut a 2 × 44-inch strip; all four borders can be cut from this one strip.

From the solid gray fabric, cut:
- 12 B triangles

  Quick-Cutting Method: Cut a 1⅞ × 44-inch strip. From the strip, cut six 1⅞-inch squares; cut each square in half diagonally to make two triangles.

- 4 A squares

  Quick-Cutting Method: Cut a 1½ × 44-inch strip. From the strip, cut four 1½-inch squares.

Piecing the Center Star

1. Join pairs of fuchsia and gray B triangles along the long sides to make squares. Make 12 pieced squares. Press the seam allowances toward the fuchsia fabric.

2. Referring to the **Fabric Key** and **Diagram 1** for correct positioning, join solid A squares and the pieced squares into four rows. Press the seam allowances in opposite directions from row to row. Join the rows to complete the center block.

Fabric Key

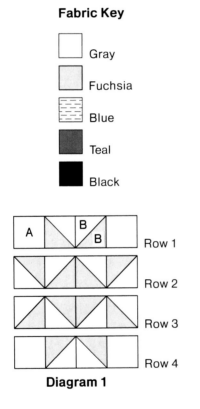

Gray

Fuchsia

Blue

Teal

Black

Diagram 1

Making the Pieced Border

1. Join pairs of black and fuchsia G triangles along the long sides to make squares. Make 24 pieced squares. Press the seam allowances toward the black fabric.

2. Referring to **Diagram 2** for positioning, sew six pieced squares into a border strip. Make four of these border strips.

Diagram 2

Assembling the Quilt Top

1. Referring to the **Quilt Diagram,** sew 1½ × 4½-inch blue C borders to two opposite sides of the center star block. Press the seam allowances away from the center of the quilt top.

2. Sew a 1½ × 6½-inch blue D border to the other two sides of the center star block. Press the seam allowances away from the center.

3. In a similar manner, add the 2 × 6½-inch teal E borders, and then the 2 × 9½-inch teal F borders. Continue to press the seam allowances away from the center of the quilt as you add the borders.

4. Sew a fuchsia and black pieced border to two opposite sides of the quilt top, making sure the tips of the black triangles point away from the center of the quilt. Add a fuchsia H square to each end of the remaining two pieced borders; sew the borders to the quilt top.

5. Add the 1¾ × 12½-inch teal I borders and the 1¾ × 15-inch teal J borders to the quilt top.

6. Sew together a 2 × 15-inch blue K border and a 2 × 15-inch black K border along one long side. Press the seam allowance toward the black border.

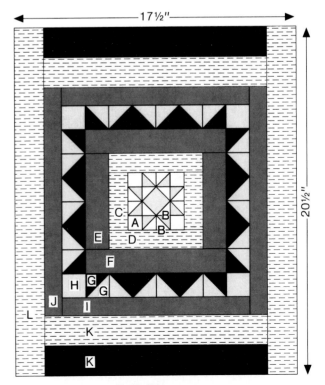

Quilt Diagram

Repeat for the other pair of K borders. Sew the K borders to the top and bottom of the quilt top, placing the black border to the outside. (In the photograph, these black borders are tucked in and are not visible.)

7. Sew the 2 × 21-inch blue L borders to the sides of the quilt top.

Quilting and Finishing

1. Mark quilting designs on the quilt top. See full-size suggested quilting designs for the borders and H squares. The pieced border is outline quilted inside each triangle.

2. Center the quilt top and batting on the quilt back and baste the layers together. Quilt all marked designs. The quilt shown was quilted with various colors of quilting thread that match the fabrics.

3. When quilting is complete, trim the batting even with the quilt top. Trim the quilt back so it is ½ inch larger all around than the quilt top. Turn in ¼ inch on the quilt back. Bring the folded edge over to the front of the quilt, covering the raw edges. Blindstitch the folded edge to the quilt top.

Quilting Design for A & B Borders

Quilting Design for H Squares

Quilting Design for Blue K Borders

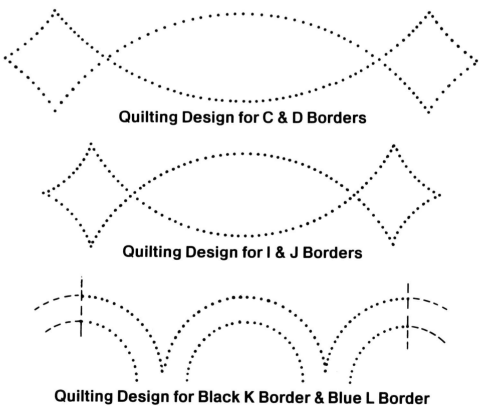

Quilting Design for C & D Borders

Quilting Design for I & J Borders

Quilting Design for Black K Border & Blue L Border

Patchwork Jewelry Roll

This pretty patchwork star is made up of pockets that hold jewelry or other small items. The pockets fasten with Velcro strips to keep your valuables from tumbling out, and the entire case rolls and ties with a ribbon to make it compact for travel.

Skill Level: Intermediate

Size: Finished roll is 14½ inches square when open; approximately 6 × 14½ inches when folded closed
Finished star block is 12 inches square

Fabrics and Supplies

- 1⅛ yards of floral print fabric
- ¼ yard of white-on-white print fabric
- ¼ yard of solid dark red fabric
- 1¼ yards of ¼-inch-wide double-faced satin ribbon
- One 16-inch square of polyester fleece
- ¼ yard of 1-inch-wide Velcro or 1 package of Velcro dots
- Rotary cutter, ruler, and mat
- Template plastic (optional)

Cutting

All measurements and patterns include ¼-inch seam allowances. The instructions below are for quick-cutting the pieces using a rotary cutter and ruler. Note that for some of the pieces, the quick-cutting method will result in leftover strips of fabric. If you prefer to cut the pieces in a traditional manner, make templates for the following pieces (measurements include ¼-inch seam allowances):

- **A:** Make a 5¼-inch square; cut the square in half diagonally in both directions.
- **B:** 4½-inch square

From the floral print fabric, cut:
- Two 16-inch squares for lining and backing
- Two 2¼ × 44-inch strips for binding
- Three 4½ × 12½-inch rectangles for the pocket linings

  Quick-Cutting Method: Cut a 4½ × 44-inch strip. From this strip, cut three 12½-inch rectangles.
- Two 1¼ × 44-inch strips for framing
- 4 B squares

  Quick-Cutting Method: Cut a 4½ × 44-inch strip. From this strip, cut four 4½-inch squares.
- 6 A triangles

  Quick-Cutting Method: Cut a 5¼ × 44-inch strip. From this strip, cut two 5¼-inch squares. Cut each square in half diagonally in both directions to make four triangles. You will have two extra triangles.

From the white-on-white print fabric, cut:
- 10 A triangles

  Quick-Cutting Method: Cut a 5¼ × 44-inch strip. From this strip, cut three 5¼-inch squares. Cut each square in half diagonally in both directions to make four triangles. You will have two extra triangles.

From the solid dark red fabric, cut:
- 4 A triangles

  Quick-Cutting Method: Cut one 5¼-inch square. Cut the square in half diagonally in both directions to make four triangles.
- Two 1 × 44-inch strips for framing

Piecing the Star Block

1. Referring to the **Fabric Key** and **Diagram 1**, join together a red and a white A triangle to make a larger triangle unit. Press the seam toward the red fabric. Make four of these units. In the same manner, join a floral triangle to a white triangle, pressing the seam toward the floral fabric. Make six of these units.

Fabric Key

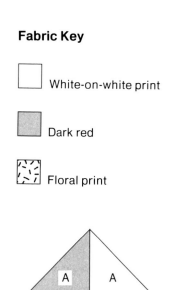

☐ White-on-white print

▨ Dark red

▦ Floral print

Diagram 1

2. Sew together a red and white triangle unit and a floral and white triangle unit to form a square, as shown in **Diagram 2.** Make a total of four of these squares.

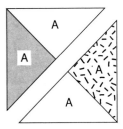

Diagram 2

3. Sew the remaining two floral and white triangle units into a square. This will form the center of the Star Block.

4. Referring to the **Piecing Diagram,** lay out the pieced squares and the 4½-inch floral B squares in three rows of three squares each. Sew the squares into rows, but do not join the rows together.

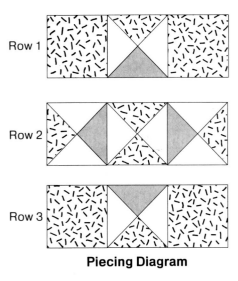

Piecing Diagram

Lining the Pockets

1. To line Row 1, place the row, right sides together, with a 4½ × 12½-inch pocket lining rectangle. Sew along both long sides of the rectangle. Turn right-side out and press. Baste the short sides closed. Repeat to line Row 2.

2. To line Row 3, place the row, right sides together, with the last pocket lining rectangle. Check

the positioning of the triangles, and sew along the edge that has the red triangle in the middle of it. Turn right-side out and press. Baste together the lower edge and side edges of the pocket and lining.

Assembling the Jewelry Roll

1. Layer the two 16-inch floral squares with the fleece square between them; the wrong sides of the floral squares should face the fleece. Baste the layers together.

2. Join a 1 × 44-inch red framing strip to a 1¼ × 44-inch floral framing strip along the long sides; press the seam toward the floral strip. Make two of these strip sets. From these strip sets, cut two 12½-inch-long segments and two 15-inch-long segments.

3. Center a 12½-inch-long strip segment along one edge of the layered 16-inch floral backing square. Place the strip right-side up on top of the square with the floral strip to the outside, and line up the long edge of the print strip with the edge of the square, as shown in **Diagram 3.** Pin in position.

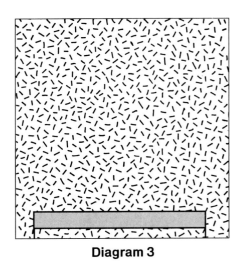

Diagram 3

4. With right sides together, center and sew the bottom raw edge of the Row 3 pocket to the top raw edge of the red strip, sewing through all layers. Flip the pocket up and pin the top edge to the background square.

5. Center the Row 2 pocket right-side up on the background square so the seams line up with the seams in Row 3; pin in position. The bottom of Row 2 should butt up against the top of Row 3. Topstitch the bottom edge of the pocket to the layered background square. Repeat for the Row 1 pocket.

6. With right sides facing, sew the red edge of the other 12½-inch-long strip set to the top of the layered square. Open out the strip and press. Your jewelry roll should look like the one shown in **Diagram 4.** Trim the excess background square that extends beyond the edge of the print strip at the top.

Trim this portion

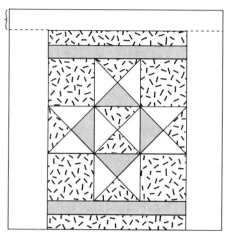

Diagram 4

7. With right sides together, align the red strip of a 15-inch strip set with the raw side edges of the three pocket rows and pin it in position. Sew through all thicknesses. Open out the strip, press, and pin it to the layered background square. Trim the background square where it extends beyond the print strip. Repeat this step on the opposite side of the square.

8. Make French-fold binding using the two 2¼-inch floral strips. Sew the strips together end to end into one long strip. Fold the strip in half lengthwise and sew it to the edges, mitering the corners. Instructions for making and attaching binding are on page 164.

9. If you would like some of the pockets divided into smaller sections, machine topstitch along the seams joining the squares. Hand stitch Velcro pieces to the pocket and foundation to hold the pockets closed. Be careful not to stitch through all the layers or your stitches will show on the outside of the jewelry roll.

10. Fold the length of ribbon in half. Hand tack the center of the ribbon to the top center of the jewelry roll back.

Blue and White Bed Set

Pull a whole room together in no time with these contemporary bedroom coordinates. Three shades of solid blue combine with muslin to create a clean, crisp look. Quick-piece the quilt from long strips of fabric. With the time you save making the quilt, stitch together the coordinating pillowcases and accent pillows from squares, rectangles, and strips.

Skill Level: Easy

About the Project Instructions

Since all of the fabric pieces needed to make these projects are strips, squares, or rectangles, no pattern pieces are given. Referring to the instructions for each project, cut the fabric pieces with a rotary cutter and a ruler, or measure and mark the pieces with a ruler and cut them with scissors. All measurements include ¼-inch seam allowances.

Striped Quilt

Size: Finished quilt is 81 × 88¾ inches

Fabrics and Supplies for the Quilt

- 4½ yards of muslin for quilt top
- 2¼ yards of solid dark blue fabric for quilt top and binding
- 5½ yards of fabric for quilt back
- Quilt batting, larger than 81 × 88¾ inches
- Rotary cutter, ruler, and mat

Cutting

Before You Begin
Divide the muslin yardage into two 81-inch (2¼-yard) pieces.

From each 81-inch piece of muslin, cut:
- Six 6 × 81-inch strips

From the solid dark blue fabric, cut:
- Eighteen 2¼ × 81-inch strips

Piecing the Quilt Top

1. Join the 12 muslin strips and 13 of the blue strips along the long sides, alternating strip colors, as shown in the **Quilt Diagram.** Refer to "Tips for Keeping Strips Straight" on page 42 for help when sewing the strips together. Press the seams toward the blue strips. Your top should measure 81 × 89¼ inches, including seam allowances.

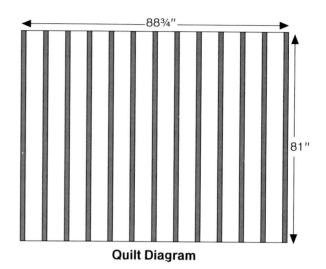

Quilt Diagram

Fabric Key

☐ Muslin

▨ Dark blue

▨ Medium blue

■ Navy

Quilting and Finishing

1. Divide the backing fabric in half into two 2¾-yard pieces. Sew the two pieces together along the long sides for the quilt back. The seam on the quilt back will run perpendicular to the stripes on the quilt front.

2. Layer the quilt back, batting, and quilt top; baste.

3. Hand or machine quilt in the ditch along all seams.

4. Make French-fold binding using the remaining five blue 81-inch strips. Sew the strips into one long strip with diagonal seams. Press the binding in half lengthwise and sew it to the quilt top, mitering the corners. Trim the excess batting and backing, and hand stitch the folded edge of the binding to the quilt back. Additional instructions for making and attaching binding are on page 164.

TIPS FOR KEEPING STRIPS STRAIGHT

To help keep the strips straight as you piece them together, try the following tips:

■ Alternate the sewing direction each time you add a strip. That is, start from a different end each time.

■ If you have a walking foot (also called an even feed foot) for your machine, try using it to sew strips together. It will help prevent curved strips.

■ Use a two-step pressing method, as shown in **Diagram A.** First, press the fabric seams just as you've sewn them, without opening out the pieces. Then, open the pieces and press the seam allowances toward the darker strips. This will give you sharp seams and precise piecing. ◆

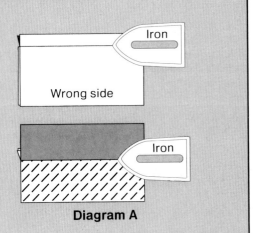

Diagram A

Pillowcases

Size: Finished pillowcases are approximately 21 × 30½ inches

Fabrics and Supplies for 2 Pillowcases

- 1½ yards of solid dark blue fabric
- 1 yard of muslin
- ½ yard of solid medium blue fabric
- 1⅝ yards of lining fabric
- Rotary cutter, ruler, and mat

Cutting

From the solid dark blue fabric, cut:
- Twenty-four 2 × 44-inch strips (12 for each case)

From the muslin, cut:
- Twenty-four 1¼ × 44-inch strips (12 for each case)

From the solid medium blue fabric, cut:
- Two 7½ × 44-inch strips (one for each case)

From the lining fabric, cut:
- Two 27½ × 42½-inch rectangles (one for each case)

Piecing the Pillowcases

1. Trim all strips so they are 42½ inches long.

2. To make one pillowcase, sew together 12 muslin and 12 dark blue strips along the long sides, alternating colors as shown in the **Pillowcase Diagram.** Refer to "Tips for Keeping Strips Straight" above for hints on sewing long strips together. Press the seams toward the dark blue strips.

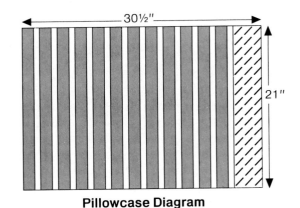

Pillowcase Diagram

3. Sew a medium blue strip to the outer muslin strip. Press the seam toward the blue strip.

4. With right sides together, sew the lining piece to the other side of the medium blue strip, leaving an opening along the seam to turn the pillowcase right-side out. Press the seam toward the medium blue strip.

5. Fold the large rectangle in half with right sides facing, as shown in **Diagram 1.** The lining section will be at one end and the striped section at the other, with the stripes folded in half. Sew the raw edges together along the three sides.

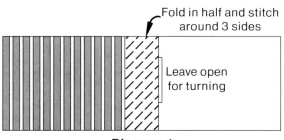

Diagram 1

6. Turn the pillowcase right-side out through the opening. Slipstitch the opening closed.

7. Smooth the lining inside the pillowcase; press. Working from the right side of the pillowcase, top-stitch along the edge of the medium blue strip to help keep the lining in place.

8. Repeat Steps 2 through 7 to make a second pillowcase.

Striped Accent Pillows

Size: Finished pillows are 10½ inches square

Fabrics and Supplies for 2 Pillows

- 1½ yards of muslin (includes fabric for pillow inserts)
- ⅔ yard of solid dark blue fabric
- Quilt batting, two 11½-inch squares
- Polyester fiberfill
- Rotary cutter, ruler, and mat

Cutting

From the muslin, cut:
- Two 9 × 12-inch rectangles for one pillow back
- Eight 11½-inch squares for pillow inserts, strip piecing foundations, and backing
- Two 1¼ × 44-inch strips
- Two 2¼ × 44-inch strips

From the solid dark blue fabric, cut:
- Two 9 × 12-inch rectangles for one pillow back
- Two 1¼ × 44-inch strips
- Two 2¼ × 44-inch strips

Stitching the Pillows

1. Refer to the **Striped Pillows Diagram.** To make the pillow with wide blue stripes and narrow muslin stripes, use the 2¼-inch blue strips and the 1¼-inch muslin strips. On an 11½-inch muslin foundation square, pin a 1¼-inch muslin strip diagonally from one corner to the opposite corner. Place a 2¼-inch blue strip atop the muslin strip, right sides together, and align one long raw edge. Stitch the blue strip to the muslin strip, sewing through all layers. Open out the blue strip and press the seam. Trim the excess muslin strips and blue strips that extend beyond the muslin square.

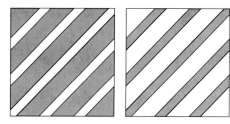

Striped Pillows Diagram

2. In a similar manner, place a muslin strip atop the blue strip, right sides together. Stitch, press, and trim. Continue to add strips, alternating colors, until the entire foundation square is covered with fabric strips.

3. Repeat Steps 1 and 2 to make a pillow top with wide muslin stripes and narrow blue stripes. Use the 2¼-inch muslin strips and 1¼-inch blue strips.

4. For each pillow, layer the pillow top (right-side up), batting, and a muslin backing square; baste. Hand or machine quilt through the middle of the wide stripes. Trim the excess backing and batting.

5. Follow the directions in "Making a Pillow with a Lapped Back" below and "Making a Pillow Insert" on the opposite page to finish the two pillows.

Square Patchwork Accent Pillow

Size: Finished pillow is 15¾ inches square

Fabrics and Supplies for 1 Pillow

- 1 yard of muslin (includes fabric for pillow insert)
- ⅔ yard of solid dark blue fabric (includes fabric for pillow back)

MAKING A PILLOW WITH A LAPPED BACK

1. To prepare the pieces for a lapped pillow back, you will need to hem one side of each pillow back rectangle. The side that is hemmed depends on the shape of the pillow. For a square pillow, hem one of the short sides of each rectangle. For a rectangular pillow, hem one of the long sides; it will be easier to slip the pillow insert into a lengthwise opening. To make the hem, turn under ¼ inch and press. Turn under ¼ inch again and topstitch the hem.

2. With right sides facing and raw edges even on three sides, pin one pillow back rectangle to the pillow front. In the same manner, pin the second pillow back rectangle to the pillow front on top of the first one, making sure that the second back is even with the edge that the first back did not cover. This way, the pillow back pieces will overlap each other. Stitch around the perimeter of the pillow, taking a ½-inch seam. Turn the pillow right-side out through the lapped pillow back opening.

3. Slip an insert into the pillow. ◆

- ⅓ yard of solid medium blue fabric
- Quilt batting, 16¾ inches square
- Polyester fiberfill
- Rotary cutter, ruler, and mat

Cutting

From the muslin, cut:
- Three 16¾-inch squares for the pillow insert and backing
- Nine 2¼-inch squares

  Quick-Cutting Method: Cut a 2¼ × 44-inch strip. From this strip, cut nine 2¼-inch squares.

From the solid dark blue fabric, cut:
- Two 10 × 17¼-inch rectangles for the pillow back
- Sixteen 3¼-inch squares

  Quick-Cutting Method: Cut two 3¼ × 44-inch strips. From this strip, cut sixteen 3¼-inch squares.

From the solid medium blue fabric, cut:
- Twenty-four 2¼ × 3¼-inch rectangles

  Quick-Cutting Method: Cut two 2¼ × 44-inch strips. Cut the strips into twenty-four 3¼-inch rectangles.

Stitching the Pillow

1. Referring to **Diagram 2,** sew together four dark blue squares and three medium blue rectangles into a row. Press the seams toward the darker fabric. Make four of these rows.

Diagram 2

2. Referring to **Diagram 3,** sew together four medium blue rectangles and three muslin squares into a row. Press the seams toward the muslin squares. Make three of these rows.

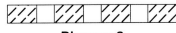

Diagram 3

3. Sew the rows together, alternating rows, as shown in the **Square Pillow Diagram.** Press the seams toward the wider rows.

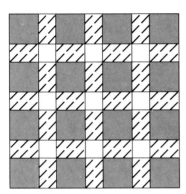

Square Pillow Diagram

4. Layer the muslin backing square, batting, and pieced top; baste. Hand or machine quilt vertically and horizontally across the pillow top in rows that intersect in the center of the dark blue squares. Trim the excess backing and batting.

5. Follow the directions in "Making a Pillow with a Lapped Back" on the opposite page and "Making a Pillow Insert" above to finish the pillow.

Rectangular Patchwork Accent Pillow

Size: Finished pillow is 12¾ × 16¼ inches

Fabrics and Supplies for 1 Pillow

- 1 yard of muslin (includes fabric for pillow back and pillow insert)
- ¼ yard of solid dark blue fabric
- ⅛ yard or scraps of solid navy fabric
- Quilt batting, 13¾ × 17¼ inches
- Polyester fiberfill
- Rotary cutter, ruler, and mat

Cutting

From the muslin, cut:
- Three 13¾ × 17¼-inch rectangles for the pillow insert and backing

MAKING A PILLOW INSERT

1. If necessary, trim the muslin pillow insert pieces so they are the same size as the pillow front.
2. Pin the insert pieces together with right sides facing. Stitch around the perimeter, taking a ½-inch seam and leaving an opening for turning and stuffing.
3. Turn the insert right-side out through the opening. Stuff the insert firmly with polyester fiberfill.
4. Hand stitch the opening closed and slip the insert into a completed pillow. ◆

- Two 10 × 17¼-inch rectangles for the pillow back
- Twenty 2¾-inch squares

  Quick-Cutting Method: Cut two 2¾ × 44-inch strips. From the strips, cut twenty 2¾-inch squares.

From the solid dark blue fabric, cut:
- Thirty-one 1¾ × 2¾-inch rectangles

  Quick-Cutting Method: Cut two 2¾-inch strips. From the strips, cut thirty-one 1¾-inch rectangles.

From the solid navy fabric, cut:
- Twelve 1¾-inch squares

  Quick-Cutting Method: Cut a 1¾ × 44-inch strip. From the strip, cut twelve 1¾-inch squares.

Stitching the Pillow

1. Sew five muslin squares and four dark blue rectangles into a row, as shown in **Diagram 4.** Press the seams toward the rectangles. Make four of these rows.

Diagram 4

2. Sew five dark blue rectangles and four navy squares into a row, as shown in **Diagram 5.** Press the seams toward the rectangles. Make three of these rows.

Diagram 5

3. Stitch the rows together, alternating the rows, as shown in the **Rectangular Pillow Diagram.** Press the seams toward the wider rows.

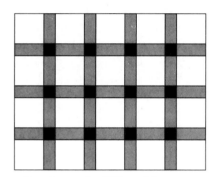

Rectangular Pillow Diagram

4. Layer the muslin backing square, batting, and pillow top (right-side up); baste. Hand or machine quilt vertically and horizontally across the pillow top in rows that intersect in the center of the muslin squares. Trim the excess backing and batting.

5. Follow the directions in "Making a Pillow with a Lapped Back" on page 44 and "Making a Pillow Insert" on page 45 to finish the pillow.

Piano Bench Cover

It would be hard to play the blues on a bright and cheerful piano bench cushion like this one. Although this project was designed as a bench cover, you could adapt it by adding a hanging sleeve to transform it into a handsome wallhanging. Solid colors like the ones shown here create a very bold look; you can soften the effect by using printed fabrics.

Skill Level: Easy

Size: Finished cushion cover is 16 × 40 inches (fits both standard and duet-size piano benches)

Finished star block is 7 inches square

Fabrics and Supplies

- ½ yard of muslin
- ½ yard of solid gold fabric
- ⅓ yard of solid rust fabric
- ¼ yard of solid navy fabric
- ⅛ yard or scraps of solid medium blue fabric
- ½ yard of backing fabric
- Quilt batting, larger than 16 × 40 inches
- Rotary cutter, ruler, and mat
- Template plastic (optional)
- 12 × 40-inch piano bench with insert. (Available through local craft shops, or write to Plain 'n Fancy Manufacturing, P.O. Box 357, Mathews, VA 23109.)

Cutting

All measurements include ¼-inch seam allowances. Instructions are given for quick-cutting the block pieces and the strips and squares that trim the star blocks. Use a rotary cutter and ruler, or measure and mark the pieces with a ruler and cut with scissors. Note that for some of the pieces, the quick-cutting method will result in leftover strips of fabric. If you prefer to cut the block pieces in a traditional manner, make templates using the measurements listed below. Instructions for making and using templates are on page 152. No patterns are given for the strips and squares that trim the blocks.

- **A:** 4-inch square
- **B:** Make a 2⅝-inch square; cut the square in half diagonally.
- **C:** Make a 4¾-inch square; cut the square in half diagonally in both directions.
- **D:** 2¼-inch square

From the muslin, cut:
- Three 1½ × 44-inch strips. Cut one strip in half to make two 22-inch strips.
- 12 C triangles

Quick-Cutting Method: Cut a 4¾ × 44-inch strip. From this strip, cut three 4¾-inch squares. Cut each square in half diagonally in both directions to make four triangles.
- 12 D squares

Quick-Cutting Method: Cut a 2¼ × 44-inch strip. From this strip, cut twelve 2¼-inch squares.

From the solid gold fabric, cut:
- Eight 3 × 7½-inch rectangles and four 3-inch squares

Quick-Cutting Method: Cut two 3 × 44-inch strips. All of these pieces can be cut from these strips.
- Two 1½ × 7½-inch rectangles and four 1½ × 3-inch rectangles

Quick-Cutting Method: Cut one 1½ × 44-inch strip. Cut off the two 7½-inch pieces, then the four 3-inch pieces.
- Reserve the remaining fabric for binding

From the solid rust fabric, cut:
- Two 1½ × 44-inch strips
- 3 A squares

Quick-Cutting Method: Cut a 4 × 44-inch strip. From the strip, cut three 4-inch squares.
- 24 B triangles

Quick-Cutting Method: Cut a 2⅝ × 44-inch strip. From the strip, cut twelve 2⅝-inch squares. Cut each square in half diagonally to make two triangles.

From the solid navy fabric, cut:
- Five 1½ × 44-inch strips. Cut one strip in half.

From the solid medium blue fabric, cut:
- One 1½ × 44-inch strip. Cut the strip in half.

Piecing the Star Blocks

1. Referring to the **Fabric Key** and **Diagram 1,** sew a rust B triangle to each short side of a muslin C triangle. Press the seams away from the muslin triangle. Make four of these units.

2. To make the top and bottom rows of the block, sew muslin D squares to the short sides of two of the BC units, as shown in **Diagram 1.** Press the seams toward the D squares.

Fabric Key

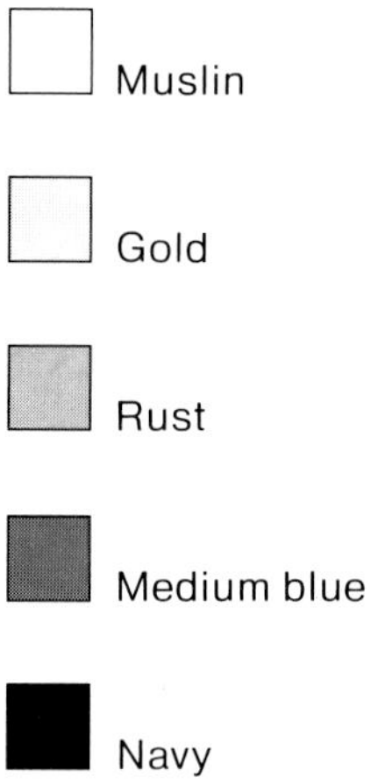

☐ Muslin

☐ Gold

▨ Rust

▨ Medium blue

■ Navy

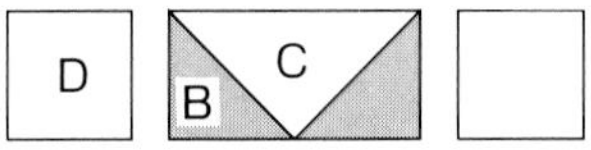

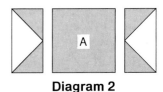

Diagram 1

3. Referring to **Diagram 2,** sew the remaining BC units to two opposite sides of a rust A square to make the middle row. Press the seams toward the center square.

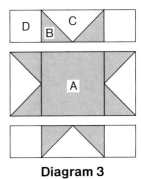

Diagram 2

4. Join the rows, referring to **Diagram 3** for correct positioning. Press the seams toward the center square.

Diagram 3

5. Repeat Steps 1 through 4 to make a total of three star blocks.

Framing the Stars

1. Sew a $1\frac{1}{2} \times 44$-inch navy strip to a $1\frac{1}{2} \times 44$-inch muslin strip along the long sides. Repeat to make a second identical 44-inch-long strip set. In the same manner, sew one half of a navy strip to one half of a muslin strip. You should now have three $2\frac{1}{2}$-inch-wide strip sets. Press the seams toward the navy strips. From these strip sets, cut 12 rectangles, each $7\frac{1}{2}$ inches long.

2. Sew one of these navy and muslin rectangles to two opposite sides of each star, as shown in **Diagram 4.** You should have six rectangles left over.

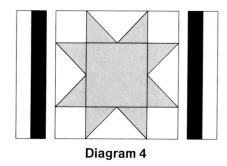

Diagram 4

3. Join the remaining half of the navy strip to one half of a medium blue strip along the long sides. You should have a strip set that is $2\frac{1}{2} \times 22$ inches. Press the seam toward the medium blue strip. From this strip set, cut 12 segments, each $1\frac{1}{2}$ inches long.

4. Sew the remaining half of the medium blue strip to the remaining half of the muslin strip to make another $2\frac{1}{2} \times 22$-inch strip set. Press the seam toward the medium blue strip. Cut 12 segments, each $1\frac{1}{2}$ inches long, from the strip set.

5. To make one corner square, sew a $1\frac{1}{2} \times 2\frac{1}{2}$-inch navy and medium blue segment to a $1\frac{1}{2} \times 2\frac{1}{2}$-inch muslin and medium blue segment, making sure the segments are positioned as shown in **Diagram 5.** Make 12 of these corner squares. Press the seams away from the muslin squares.

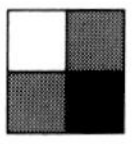

Diagram 5

6. Sew a corner square to both short sides of the six navy and muslin rectangles left over from Step 2, positioning the squares as shown in **Diagram 6.** Sew these units to the remaining two sides of all the star blocks.

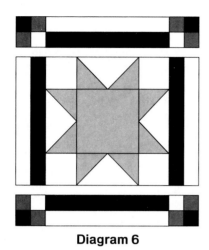

Diagram 6

Assembling the Quilt Top

1. Sew a 1½ × 44-inch rust strip to a 1½ × 44-inch navy strip along the long sides. Press the seam toward the navy strip. Repeat to make a second identical strip set. From the strip sets, cut sixteen 3-inch-long rectangles and four 1½-inch-long segments.

2. Sew the 2½ × 3-inch rust and navy rectangles to both short sides of the eight 3 × 7½-inch gold rectangles, as shown in **Diagram 7.** Press the seams toward the gold rectangles. Sew six of these units to opposite sides of the three framed star blocks. Press the seams away from the center of the block. Sew a 3-inch gold square to both short sides of the two remaining units. These will become the end rows of the quilt.

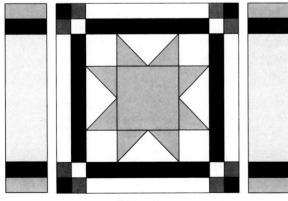

Diagram 7

3. Make a narrow row by sewing 1½ × 2½-inch rust and navy segments to the short sides of a 1½ × 7½-inch gold rectangle. Add a 1½ × 3-inch gold rectangle to each end. Repeat to make a second narrow row.

4. Assemble the rows, as shown in the **Piecing Diagram.**

Piecing Diagram

Quilting and Finishing

1. Layer the backing, batting, and quilt top; baste.

2. Hand or machine quilt ¼ inch from the seams around the stars. Quilt through the center of all the narrow strips and small squares. Add additional lines of quilting in the larger gold pieces.

3. Make French-fold binding from the remaining gold fabric. You will need approximately 121 inches (3⅜ yards) of binding. Finish the outside edges with the binding, mitering the corners. Instructions for making and attaching binding are on page 164. Instructions for making and attaching a hanging sleeve are on page 167.

4. To install the cover, loosen the screws on the back side of the insert and remove it from the bench lid. Center the quilt on the insert and wrap the edges around to the back. Secure the quilt in position by loosely basting together the overlapped edges on the back side of the insert. Replace the insert in the bench lid and tighten the screws.

Log Cabin
Purse Accessories

Show off your patchwork talents each time you reach into your purse. Turn miniature Log Cabin blocks into a charming set of accessories that includes a key ring, eyeglass case, and checkbook cover. Dig into your scrap bag to come up with an assortment of coordinating fabrics.

Skill Level: Intermediate

Size: Finished eyeglass case and checkbook cover are approximately 3¾ × 7¼ inches
Finished key ring is approximately 2¼ inches square
Finished Log Cabin blocks are 1¾ inches square

Fabrics and Supplies

- ½ yard of coordinating print fabric for trim, backs, and linings
- ⅛ yard of solid black fabric for trim
- Scraps of solid rose fabric for the centers of the blocks
- Scraps of at least six light print fabrics *and* six dark print fabrics for the Log Cabin blocks
- ¼ yard of polyester fleece
- ⅛ yard or scraps of mid-weight fusible interfacing
- Scrap of ⅛-inch-wide black satin ribbon
- Rotary cutter, ruler, and mat
- 1 key ring

Cutting

All measurements include ¼-inch seam allowances. There are no patterns for the pieces; cut the pieces with a rotary cutter and ruler or measure them with a ruler and cut with scissors. You will need a total of seven Log Cabin blocks to make the three items in the set. Following the instructions below, determine the placement of your fabrics and then cut all of the strips for the blocks at the same time.

From the print fabric, cut:
- Four 1¼ × 6¼-inch strips and four 1¼ × 4¼-inch strips

  Quick-Cutting Method: Cut a 1¼ × 44-inch strip. You should be able to cut all of the pieces from this strip.
- One 1¼ × 44-inch strip for binding
- Reserve the remaining fabric for lining and backing

From the solid black fabric, cut:
- Four ¾ × 5¾-inch strips and four ¾ × 2¾-inch strips

Quick-Cutting Method: Cut a ¾ × 44-inch strip. You should be able to cut all of the pieces from this strip.

From the solid rose fabric, cut:
- Seven ½-inch squares for the centers of the blocks

From the assorted scrap light and dark print fabrics, cut:
- One ½-inch-wide strip from each fabric. Referring to the photograph and the **Log Cabin Block Diagram,** determine the placement of your fabrics. You can use the same fabrics in every block, or add fabrics and mix them up to make different but coordinated blocks. Then cut the strips to length according to the **Cutting Chart.** Cut seven of each number, one for each of the seven blocks. Make labels from 1 to 12 and pin a label to each pile of strips as you cut them.

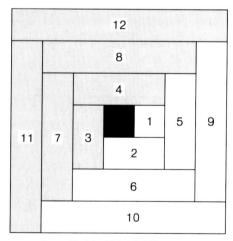

Log Cabin Block Diagram

CUTTING CHART

Strip Number	Length of ½-Inch Strip
1	½ inch
2 & 3	1 inch
4 & 5	1¼ inches
6 & 7	1½ inches
8 & 9	1¾ inches
10 & 11	2 inches
12	2¼ inches

Piecing the Blocks

1. The most efficient way to piece the blocks is to do the same step for all seven at one time in assembly-line fashion. Take accurate ¼-inch seams when sewing. Press seam allowances away from the block center and trim the seam allowances to ⅛ inch. Begin by sewing a Strip 1 to the center rose square, as shown in **Diagram 1.** Repeat for a total of seven blocks.

Diagram 1

2. Sew Strip 2 to the long side of the Step 1 unit, as shown in **Diagram 2.** Press and trim as in Step 1. Repeat for all the blocks.

Diagram 2

3. Referring to the **Log Cabin Block Diagram,** continue to add numbered strips in order around the center until all 12 strips have been added. Complete all seven blocks. The completed blocks should measure 2¼ inches, including seam allowances.

4. Referring to **Diagram 3,** sew together three blocks into a rectangle for the eyeglass case. Repeat for the checkbook cover. The remaining block is for the key ring.

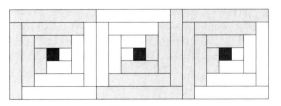

Diagram 3

Piecing the Fronts of the Eyeglass Case and Checkbook Cover

1. Sew the ¾ × 5¾-inch black strips to the long sides of the assembled rectangles; press the seams toward the black strips. Sew the ¾ × 2¾-inch black strips to the short sides of the rectangles; press the seams toward the black strips.

2. In the same manner, sew the 1¼ × 6¼-inch print strips to the long sides of the rectangles. Press the seams toward the print strips. Sew the 1¼ × 4¼-inch print strips to the short sides. Press the seams toward the print strips.

Assembling the Eyeglass Case

1. Cut a piece of fleece that is 1 inch larger on all sides than one of the rectangles from Step 2 above. Layer the fleece under the Log Cabin rectangle. Machine quilt between the Log Cabin blocks and around the inside of the black border strips to secure the fabric to the fleece. Trim the excess fleece even with the edge of the rectangle.

2. Measure the assembled front of the eyeglass case. It should measure approximately 4¼ × 7¾ inches. Using these measurements, cut three rectangles from the reserved print fabric.

3. Pin one print rectangle, right sides together, to the assembled front. Using a ¼-inch seam, stitch together on two long sides and one short side. Turn right-side out and press.

4. For the lining, place the two remaining print rectangles right sides together. Sew together on three sides, leaving a short side unsewn. Turn right-side out and press.

5. Slip the lining inside the case. Turn in ¼ inch along the top raw edges of the lining and the case. Machine topstitch the edges together near the folds. Turn the case inside out and tack the lining to the case at the bottom corners to keep it from pulling out.

Assembling the Checkbook Cover

1. Measure the assembled front. It should measure approximately 4¼ × 7¾ inches. Using these measurements, cut three rectangles from the remaining print fabric. Set aside two of the rectangles.

2. With right sides together, sew one print rectangle to a long side of the assembled front. Open out to make a large square.

3. Measure the square. It should measure approximately 7¾ × 8 inches. Using these measurements, cut a piece of fleece and a piece of print fabric. Layer the assembled square and the print backing with the fleece between them; the wrong sides of the front and back should be facing the fleece. Machine quilt between the Log Cabin blocks and around the inside of the black border strips to secure the layers.

4. Cut two 3-inch-wide strips of interfacing the same length as the two remaining print rectangles. Fuse the interfacing to the wrong side of the fabric rectangles, aligning the interfacing with one long edge and two short edges. These are the flaps.

5. To hem the flaps, fold over ½ inch along the noninterfaced long edge on each rectangle and press, as shown in **Diagram 4.** Fold again along the line created by the interfacing. Machine topstitch the hems. The flaps should measure 3 inches by approximately 7¾ inches.

6. Place the flaps right-side up on the wrong side (the inside) of the checkbook cover. Place one at each end, aligning the raw edges on three sides with the raw edges of the cover. Baste the edges of the flaps to the edges of the cover.

7. Use the remaining 1¼-inch strip of print fabric to bind the outer edges, mitering the corners. Instructions for making and attaching binding are on page 164.

Assembling the Key Ring

1. Cut a piece of fleece ¼ inch larger on all sides than the Log Cabin block.

2. Cut a piece of print backing ½ inch larger on all sides than the block.

3. Layer the backing and the block with the fleece between them; the wrong sides of the front and back should be facing the fleece. Machine quilt in the ditch to secure the layers.

4. Turn under ¼ inch on the backing fabric. Bring the folded edges to the front, concealing the raw edges of the fleece and block. Blindstitch the folded edges to the quilt block. Before stitching down the last edge, make a ½-inch ribbon loop to hold the key ring and stitch it to one corner of the square so that the ends will be covered by the folded edge. Blindstitch the last folded edge in place.

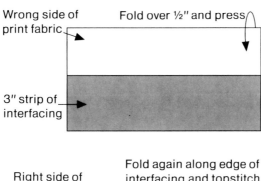

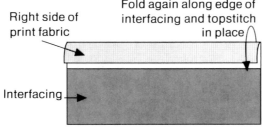

Diagram 4

Calico Star
Room Accessories

Here's a quick-and-easy pair that brings country cheer to any room. The Wall Pockets keep things like keys, scissors, and stationery handy, and the Tissue Box Cover adds a nice coordinated touch. The stars are actually machine appliquéd as a single piece, so construction is a breeze. Whip them up in different colors for perfect gifts!

Skill Level: Easy

Size: Finished Wall Pockets hanging is 17 × 25 inches
Tissue Box Cover is 4½ inches wide on each side and 5¼ inches tall

Fabrics and Supplies for Wall Pockets

- 1 yard of medium blue print fabric for stars, borders, and backing
- ½ yard of light pink print fabric for sashing strips and pocket linings
- ½ yard of muslin for background of stars and pocket foundations
- Two 5-inch or larger squares *each* of purple and light green print fabrics for stars
- Paper-backed fusible webbing, such as Wonder-Under
- Machine appliqué fabric stabilizer, such as Tear-Away
- ½ yard of fusible fleece, such as Pellon
- ¼-inch-diameter wooden dowel, approximately 16 inches long
- ⅔ yard of ⅝-inch-wide ribbon
- Rotary cutter, ruler, and mat
- Thread to match the appliqué fabrics

Cutting

All measurements include ¼-inch seam allowances. The pattern for the star is on page 60. Do not cut the stars out at this time; you will cut them out later, during the construction of the pockets.

From the medium blue print fabric, cut:
- One 19 × 27-inch backing rectangle
- Two 2½ × 25½-inch side border strips and two 2½ × 13½-inch top and bottom border strips
- Reserve the remaining fabric for stars

From the light pink print fabric, cut:
- Three 7½ × 13½-inch pocket lining rectangles
- Six 1½ × 13½-inch sashing strips
- Nine 1½ × 5½-inch sashing strips

From the muslin, cut:
- Six 5½-inch background squares
- One 13½ × 21½-inch rectangle for pocket foundation

Making the Star Blocks

Construct the star blocks in three horizontal pocket rows with two stars per row.

1. Sew together three 1½ × 5½-inch pink strips and two 5½-inch muslin squares, as shown in **Diagram 1**. Press the seams toward the pink strips. Add a 1½ × 13½-inch pink sashing strip to the top and bottom of the unit to complete the row. Again, press the seams toward the pink strips. The row should measure 7½ × 13½ inches, including seam allowances. Make a total of three rows exactly like this one.

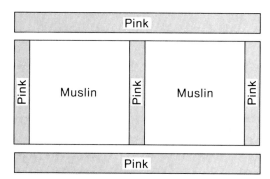

Diagram 1

2. Place a row, right sides together, with a 7½ × 13½-inch pink pocket lining rectangle. Sew together along the long top and bottom edges. Turn right-side out and press. Repeat for a second row. For the third row, sew only along the top edge, turn to the right side, and press.

3. Trace six stars on the paper side of the fusible webbing, using the **Large Star Pattern** on page 60. Do not add seam allowances. Cut loosely around the stars; do not cut on the lines at this point. Following the manufacturer's directions, fuse two stars each to the blue, green, and purple fabric scraps for a total of six stars. Cut out the stars on the cutting lines. For tips on appliquéing with fusible webbing, see page 158.

4. Remove the paper backing from the stars. Center and fuse the stars onto the muslin background squares on all three rows.

5. Place stabilizer under the wrong side of the pockets. Machine appliqué the stars to the background squares. Begin by stitching the vertical, horizontal, and diagonal intersecting lines shown on the pattern. Then stitch around the perimeter of each star. See page 158 for suggestions on machine appliqué.

Assembling the Pockets

1. Placing right sides together, sew a 2½ × 13½-inch blue border strip to a short side of the 13½ × 21½-inch muslin pocket foundation. Press the seam allowance toward the strip. This will become the top of the wallhanging.

2. Position and pin the first star pocket row on the right side of the foundation. Butt the top of the pocket row against the bottom edge of the blue border strip, as shown in **Diagram 2**. Align the raw edges of the pink side strips with the raw edges of the muslin foundation. To attach the pocket, topstitch across the bottom of the row, about ⅛ inch from the lower edge of the pink strip.

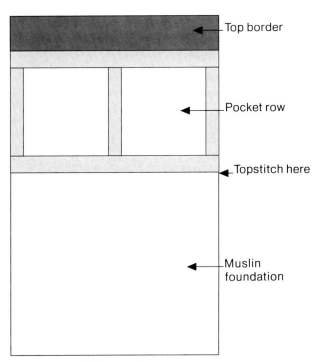

Diagram 2

3. Position and pin the second pocket row in the same manner. The top of the row should butt up against the bottom of the first row. Topstitch across

the bottom of the row, ⅛ inch from the lower edge of the pink strip.

4. Position the bottom pocket row on the muslin foundation and pin in place. Again, the top of the row should butt up against the bottom of the row above it. With right sides together, sew a 2½ × 13½-inch blue border strip to the lower edge of the row, stitching through all thicknesses and securing the row to the foundation. Press the seam allowance toward the border strip.

5. Trim any excess muslin foundation. Measure the long sides of the wallhanging, including top and bottom borders. If necessary, trim the 2½ × 25½-inch blue side border strips to this length. Placing right sides together, sew a blue border strip to each side of the wallhanging top. Press the seams toward the borders.

Assembling and Finishing the Wall Pockets

1. Measure the assembled front. Trim the blue backing rectangle to size. Cut a piece of fusible fleece to the same size.

2. Position the wrong side of the backing rectangle against the fusible side of the fleece; fuse, following the manufacturer's instructions.

3. Place the wallhanging top right sides together with the back; pin. Using a ¼-inch seam, sew the two together, leaving a 5-inch opening along the bottom edge for turning. Clip the corners after sewing. Turn right-side out through the opening and hand stitch the opening closed.

4. Topstitch down the center of the center pink strips to form the six pockets. Stitch in the ditch along the outside edges and across the bottom of the pink strips.

5. Make a hanging sleeve. Instructions for making hanging sleeves are on page 167.

Fabrics and Supplies for the Tissue Box Cover

- ¼ yard of cream print fabric for cover
- Four 5-inch or larger squares of print fabric for stars
- Plastic-coated freezer paper

- Lightweight quilt batting or polyester fleece, 10 × 20 inches
- Paper-backed fusible webbing, such as Wonder-Under
- Boutique-type box of facial tissues
- Rotary cutter, ruler, and mat

Making the Cover

1. Referring to the dimensions in **Diagram 3,** make a freezer paper pattern for the cover. Do not add seam allowances.

2. Fold the cream print fabric in half, selvage to selvage, with right sides together. Using a dry iron on the wool setting, press the freezer paper pattern to the wrong side of the fabric, leaving at least ¼ inch of fabric around the edges for seam allowances.

3. Pin the folded fabric, with pattern attached, to the fleece, keeping the pattern side facing up. Stitch around the edge of the pattern, stitching through both layers of fabric and the fleece. Leave an opening at one end as indicated on the pattern.

4. Remove the paper pattern. Clip the corners. Turn right-side out through the opening and hand stitch the opening closed. Machine topstitch as indicated on the pattern.

5. Using the **Small Star Pattern** on page 60, trace four stars onto the paper side of the fusible webbing. Loosely cut out around the stars; do not cut on the lines yet. Following the manufacturer's instructions for using fusible web, fuse the stars to the four 5-inch squares of print fabric. Cut out the stars on the cutting line.

6. Remove the paper backing. Center and fuse a star to each section of the tissue box cover.

7. Place stabilizer under the background fabric. Machine appliqué the stars to the background. Begin by stitching the vertical, horizontal, and diagonal intersecting lines marked on the pattern. Then stitch around the perimeter of the star.

8. Fold the cover around the box of tissues; pin together. Hand stitch the top flaps to the sides first, then stitch the seam along the side.

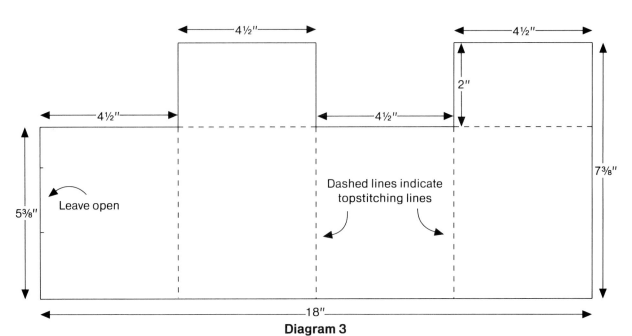

Diagram 3

Pattern for Tissue Box Cover

Large Star Pattern

Machine appliqué
along these lines

Machine appliqué along these lines

Small Star Pattern

Country Aprons

These down-home favorites are as pretty as they are practical. The skirts attach to the bibs with snaps, so you can mix and match the tops and bottoms to create nine different combinations. Quick-cutting and quick-piecing make these aprons go together in a jiffy.

Skill Level: Intermediate

Size: One size fits most adults
Apron skirt is 20 inches long

Fabrics and Supplies for the Star Apron
(In the center in the photo)

- 1¼ yards of floral print fabric for the apron skirt, bib lining, and star block. (Purchase additional fabric if you wish to cut the skirt longer.)
- ½ yard of solid navy fabric for bib trim, neckband, and patchwork
- ¼ yard or scraps of muslin for patchwork
- One 12-inch square of polyester fleece or other low-loft batting
- 4 pairs of sew-on snaps
- Rotary cutter, ruler, and mat
- Template plastic (optional)

Cutting

Measurements for all pieces include ¼-inch seam allowances. The instructions are for quick-cutting the pieces with a rotary cutter and ruler. Note that for some of the pieces, the quick-cutting method may result in leftover strips of fabric. If you prefer to cut the pieces in a traditional manner, make templates for the following pieces (measurements include ¼-inch seam allowances):

- **A:** Make a 1⅞-inch square; cut the square in half diagonally.
- **B:** 1½-inch square
- **C:** 2½-inch square
- **D:** 1½ × 4½-inch rectangle
- **E:** 1½ × 2½-inch rectangle

From the floral print fabric, cut:

- One 21 × 44-inch piece for the apron skirt. Cut this piece longer than 21 inches if you want a longer skirt on your apron.
- Two 2½ × 44-inch strips for the apron waistband/ties
- 16 A triangles

  Quick-Cutting Method: Cut a 1⅞ × 44-inch strip. From this strip, cut eight 1⅞-inch squares. Cut each square in half diagonally to make two triangles.

- 4 D rectangles

  Quick-Cutting Method: Cut a 1½ × 44-inch strip. From this strip, cut four 1½ × 4½-inch rectangles.

- Reserve the remaining fabric for the bib back

From the solid navy fabric, cut:

- One 2½ × 44-inch strip for the neckband
- One 2½ × 10-inch strip for the top bib trim
- One 3 × 10-inch strip for the bottom bib trim
- 1 C square

  Quick-Cutting Method: Cut one 2½-inch square.

- 12 B squares

  Quick-Cutting Method: Cut a 1½ × 44-inch strip. From this strip, cut twelve 1½-inch squares.

- 16 A triangles

  Quick-Cutting Method: Cut a 1⅞ × 44-inch strip. From this strip, cut eight 1⅞-inch squares; cut each square in half diagonally to make two triangles.

From the muslin, cut:

- 4 E rectangles

  Quick-Cutting Method: Cut a 1½ × 44-inch strip. From this strip, cut four 1½ × 2½-inch rectangles.

- 8 B squares

  Quick-Cutting Method: Cut a 1½ × 44-inch strip. From this strip, cut eight 1½-inch squares.

Sewing the Skirt

1. Press under ¼ inch along one long side and two short sides of the skirt. Press under 1-inch-wide hems along these three edges. Hand or machine stitch the hems. The long side will become the bottom of the skirt and the two short sides will be the sides of the skirt.

2. Sew together the short sides of the 2½ × 44-inch waistband/tie strips to make one long piece. Press the seam open. Place a pin approximately 10 inches to each side of this center seam to mark the length of the waistband.

3. Fold the skirt in half to find the center of the raw top edge, and mark it with a pin. Using two rows of stitching, machine baste along the top edge. Gather the top edge of the skirt to fit the waistband (approximately 20 inches). Pin the right side of one edge of the waistband to the right side of the gathered skirt, aligning the raw edges. Match the center of the band to the center of the skirt and the side edges of the skirt to the pins marking the ends of the waistband section. Adjust the gathers and sew the waistband to the skirt.

4. Try the apron on to determine the length of the ties. Twenty-eight inches or so is a good length for the ties, but you can choose to leave them longer or trim them even shorter than that.

5. Fold the tie portions of the strip in half lengthwise with right sides facing. Stitch across the ends of the ties and along the length, ending the stitching when you reach the edge of the skirt. Turn the ties right-side out and press.

6. Turn under ¼ inch on the raw edge of the waistband section. Hand stitch the edge of the band to the wrong side of the skirt.

Piecing the Bib

1. Sew a navy A triangle to a floral print A triangle to form a square. Press the seam toward the navy triangle. Make a total of 16 of these squares.

2. Referring to the **Fabric Key** and **Diagram 1,** sew eight of the squares together in pairs along the floral print edges so the floral print triangles form a larger triangle. You will have four rectangular units. These rectangular units will form the center star.

Fabric Key

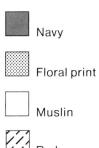

Navy

Floral print

Muslin

Red

Diagram 1

3. Sew a rectangular unit from Step 2 to two opposite sides of the navy C square, as shown in **Diagram 2.** Sew a muslin B square to each short side of the other two rectangular units. Join these to the remaining two sides of the C square, as shown, to make the center star.

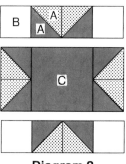

Diagram 2

4. Sew a floral print D rectangle to two opposite sides of the center star, as shown in **Diagram 3.** Sew a navy B square to the short ends of the two remaining D rectangles. Sew these strips to the remaining two sides of the star, as shown.

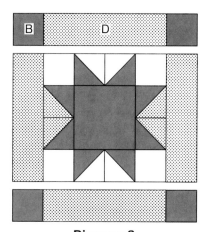

Diagram 3

5. Sew together the eight remaining squares from Step 1 in pairs. This time, stitch along the navy edges so the navy triangles form a larger triangle. You will have four rectangular units.

6. Referring to **Diagram 4,** sew a navy B square to the short sides of each Step 5 unit.

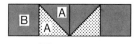

Diagram 4

7. Add a muslin B square to each end of two of the units. Sew the units to two opposite sides of the center star, as shown in **Diagram 5.**

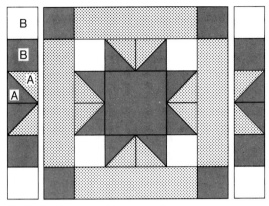

Diagram 5

8. Add a muslin E rectangle to each end of the remaining two units. Referring to **Diagram 6,** sew the units to the remaining two sides of the center star to complete the block.

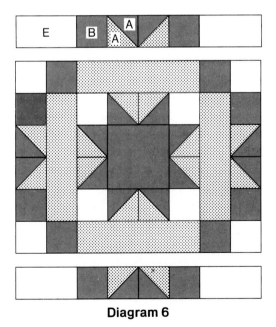

Diagram 6

Finishing the Bib

1. From the excess apron fabric, cut a backing piece that is 2 inches larger on all sides than the pieced block. Cut a matching piece of batting.

2. Layer the backing fabric, batting, and block; baste. Quilt as desired.

3. Trim the batting and backing so they are 1 inch larger than the block at the top and side edges and 1½ inches larger at the bottom edge.

4. To trim the bottom edge of the bib, pin the 3 × 10-inch bottom trim strip, right sides together, to the bottom edge of the block, and sew through all layers. Press the seam allowance toward the trim strip. Turn under ¼ inch along the long raw edge of the trim strip. Bring the folded edge to the back of the bib and hand stitch in place.

5. To trim the top edge of the bib, pin the 2½ × 10-inch top trim strip, right sides together, to the top edge of the bib, and sew through all layers. Turn under ¼ inch along the long raw edge of the trim strip. Bring the folded edge to the back of the bib and hand stitch in place.

6. Use the 2½ × 44-inch neckband strip to finish the side edges and form the neckband. First, turn under ¼ inch along each long side and press.

7. Open out the pressed edge on one of the long sides. Leaving ¼ inch extending at the bottom bib edge, pin one end of the strip to one side of the bib, with right sides facing and the unfolded raw edge of the strip aligned with the raw edge of the bib. Try the apron on, adjust the length of the neckband as needed, and pin the other end of the strip to the other side edge. If necessary, trim the end of the strip to ¼ inch beyond the bottom of the bib. Sew the strip to both apron sides, stitching along the fold line.

8. Turn in the seam allowance at both ends of the strip and press. Along the apron sides, fold the turned-under edges (the long edges of the neckband strip) in half, bring them to the bib back, and hand stitch in place. Hand stitch the openings at the bottom edges of the bib.

9. Hand or machine stitch the turned edges together along the neckband section.

10. To attach the bib to the skirt, stitch the socket sections of four snaps along the lower edge of the bib so they are evenly spaced. Stitch the prong sections of the snaps in matching positions on the inside of the waistband on the apron skirt.

Fabrics and Supplies for the Seminole Bib

(On the right in the photo)

- 1¼ yards of solid navy fabric for the apron skirt, bib lining, and patchwork. (Purchase additional fabric if you wish to cut the skirt longer.)

- ½ yard of solid red fabric for bib trim, neckband, and patchwork
- ¼ yard or scraps of muslin for patchwork
- One 12-inch square of polyester fleece or other low-loft batting
- 4 pairs of sew-on snaps
- Rotary cutter, ruler, and mat
- Template plastic (optional)

Cutting

Measurements for all pieces include ¼-inch seam allowances. There are no pattern pieces for this bib. Seminole patchwork is done by sewing together strips of fabric into a strip set. The set is then cut into smaller segments that are joined to create the design. Use a rotary cutter and ruler to cut all the strips and pieces.

From the solid navy fabric, cut:
- One 21 × 44-inch piece for the apron skirt. (Cut this piece longer than 21 inches if you want a longer skirt on your apron.)
- Two 2½ × 44-inch strips for the apron waistband/ties
- Two ¾ × 44-inch strips for patchwork
- One ¾ × 10-inch strip for patchwork
- Reserve the remaining fabric for the bib back

From the solid red fabric, cut:
- One 2½ × 44-inch strip for the neckband
- Two 1¾ × 44-inch strips for patchwork
- One 3 × 10-inch strip for the bottom bib trim
- One 2½ × 10-inch strip for the top bib trim
- One 1⅛ × 10-inch strip for patchwork

From the muslin, cut:
- Two 1¾ × 44-inch strips for patchwork
- Two 1¼ × 44-inch strips for patchwork
- One 1¼ × 10-inch strip for patchwork
- One 1 × 10-inch strip for patchwork

Sewing the Skirt

Using the navy fabric, make the apron skirt according to the instructions in "Sewing the Skirt" on page 62.

Piecing the Bib

1. Referring to the **Fabric Key** and **Diagram 7,** sew 44-inch-long strips together in the following order to make a strip set: 1¾-inch muslin, ¾-inch navy, 1¼-inch muslin, and 1¾-inch red. Press the seam allowances to one side. Repeat to make a second identical strip set.

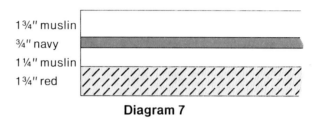

1¾" muslin
¾" navy
1¼" muslin
1¾" red

Diagram 7

2. Place the two strip sets, right sides facing, with raw edges aligned. Align the 45 degree angle mark on your ruler with the bottom of the strip set. Trim the end of the strip set at a 45 degree angle, as shown in **Diagram 8,** cutting through both layers.

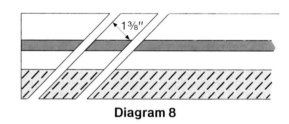

1⅜"

Diagram 8

3. Referring to **Diagram 8,** cut 1⅜-inch-wide segments from the layered strip sets, making cuts parallel to the angled edge. You will get two mirror-image segments each time you cut. Cut 10 pairs of segments. Leave the segments grouped in mirror-image pairs.

4. Sew each pair of segments together as shown in **Diagram 9.** You will have 10 units.

Diagram 9

5. Make a pieced strip by sewing together five of the units, as shown in **Diagram 10.** Make a second identical strip.

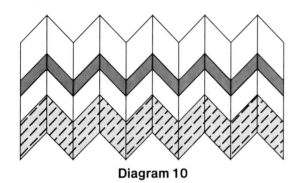

Diagram 10

6. Referring to **Diagram 11,** trim the strips along the muslin edge, creating a straight edge with approximately ¼ inch for seam allowance beyond the navy peaks. Trim the strips along the red edge as shown, creating a straight edge with approximately ½ inch for seam allowance below the lowest points on the muslin strip.

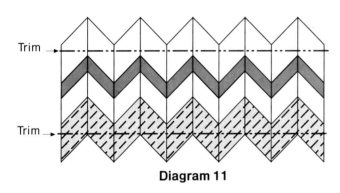

Diagram 11

7. Sew the patchwork strips together along the red edges, taking a ¼-inch seam.

8. Sew the 10-inch strips together in the following order: 1⅛-inch-wide red, 1¼-inch-wide muslin, navy, and 1-inch-wide muslin. Press the seams to one side.

9. Sew the red edge of the Step 8 strip set to one side of the Seminole patchwork section. Press the seam toward the red strip. Trim the ends of the strip set even with the sides of the patchwork. The pieced bib should measure approximately 9¼ inches wide and 7½ inches high.

10. Using the red fabric, finish the bib following the instructions given in "Finishing the Bib" on page 64.

Fabrics and Supplies for the Pine Tree Bib
(On the left in the photo)

- 1¼ yards of muslin for the apron skirt, bib lining, and patchwork. (Purchase additional fabric if you wish to cut the skirt longer.)
- ½ yard of green print fabric for the bib trim, neckband, and patchwork
- ¼ yard or scraps of assorted green, red, and light brown printed fabrics for the patchwork trees
- One 12-inch square of polyester fleece or other low-loft batting
- 4 pairs of sew-on snaps
- Plastic-coated freezer paper to make templates for the tree blocks
- Rotary cutter, ruler, and mat
- Template plastic (optional)

Cutting

This bib consists of four different 4-inch-square tree blocks sewn together into a larger block. You could simplify the bib by making all four blocks the same. Cut the pieces listed here, then follow the directions below for cutting the pieces for the tree blocks. These measurements include ¼-inch seam allowances.

From the muslin, cut:
- One 21 × 44-inch piece for the apron skirt. Cut this piece longer than 21 inches if you want a longer skirt on your apron.
- Two 2½ × 44-inch strips for the apron waistband/ties
- Reserve the remaining fabric for the bib back

From the green print fabric, cut:
- One 2½ × 44-inch strip for the neckband
- One 3 × 14-inch strip for the bib bottom trim
- One 2½ × 14-inch strip for the bib top trim

Sewing the Skirt

Using the muslin, make the skirt according to the instructions in "Sewing the Skirt" on page 62.

Preparing the Block Pieces

The instructions for cutting the pieces for the tree blocks use a special technique that makes templates from freezer paper. Each template set can be used only once to make a single block. If you plan to make multiples of any blocks, you will need to make a separate set of paper templates for each one. Full-size patterns for the tree blocks appear on pages 68 and 69. Refer to the patterns as you piece the blocks.

This template method can be used to make all of the block pieces except the tree (Pattern Piece 2) in Block D. Follow the instructions below to piece that tree.

1. To make the templates for a tree block, trace the full-size pattern onto the uncoated side of a piece of freezer paper. Use a ruler to help you draw straight lines.

2. Transfer the pattern piece numbers onto your drawing. All of the blocks are assembled in numerical order. Label each piece according to the fabric from which you wish to cut it. For example, for Block A, label Pieces 2, 5, and 8 green for the tree.

3. Cut out the drawing of the block. Then cut the block apart on all the drawn lines. You will have one paper template for each piece in the block.

4. Place the coated side of each paper template atop the wrong side of the fabric you have chosen for that piece. Allow at least a ½-inch margin between the individual pieces to allow for seam allowances. With a dry iron set at a medium setting, press the paper pieces to the wrong sides of the fabrics.

5. Cut out each piece, allowing a ¼-inch seam allowance around all sides. Use a rotary cutter and ruler, or mark the seam allowance with a ruler and cut the pieces with scissors. Leave the paper attached to the wrong side of the fabric pieces until the entire block is assembled. The edges of the paper pieces will serve as stitching guides, and the numbers on the paper will aid you in assembling the blocks.

Piecing Blocks A and B

1. The assembly for these two blocks is the same. Piece them in four horizontal rows. To make the first row, pin Piece 1 to Piece 2, right sides together. Stitch the pieces together, sewing along the edges of the paper templates on the wrong side of

the fabric. Press the seam allowances to one side. Sew Piece 3 to the other side of Piece 2 and press.

2. Piece the other three rows in a similar manner.

3. Join the rows to complete the block. Peel off the freezer paper.

Piecing Block C

1. To make the patchwork tree, sew together Pieces 1, 2, 3, and 4 in numerical order.

2. Sew Piece 5 and Piece 6 to the sides of the tree.

3. Join together Pieces 7, 8, and 9 to make the trunk row.

4. Join the tree section to the trunk section to complete the block.

Piecing Block D

1. Pattern Piece 2 (the tree) for this block is cut from fabric pieced from strips. To make the pieced fabric, begin by cutting a total of seven 1 × 4-inch strips from assorted tree fabrics.

2. Sew the long sides of the fabric strips together to create the pieced fabric. Press the seams to one side.

3. Press the paper template for Piece 2 to the wrong side of the pieced fabric. Cut out the piece, allowing ¼-inch seam allowances on all sides.

4. Sew together Piece 1 and Piece 2; then add Piece 3.

5. Sew together Pieces 4, 5, and 6 to make the trunk row.

6. Join the trunk row to the tree section to complete the block.

Completing the Patchwork Section

1. Lay out the blocks in a pleasing arrangement. Sew the blocks into two rows of two blocks each. Join the two rows to complete the block.

2. Using the green print fabric, finish the bib following the instructions in "Finishing the Bib" on page 64.

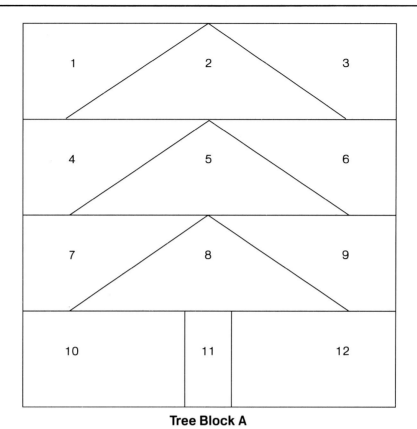

Tree Block A

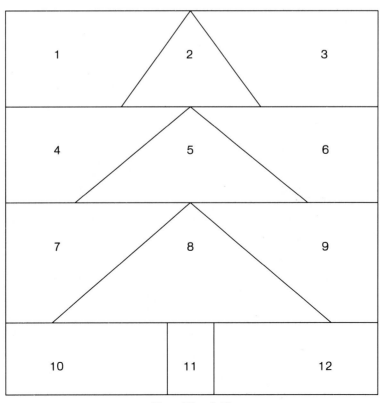

Tree Block B

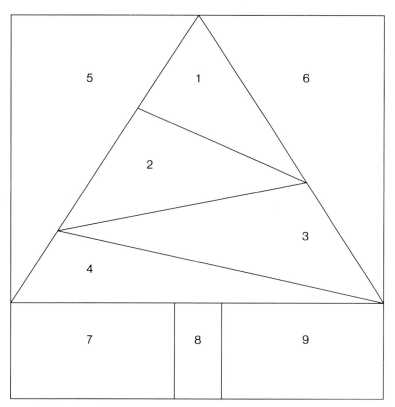

Tree Block C

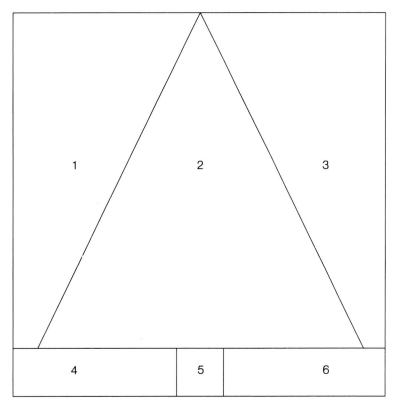

Tree Block D

GARDEN DELIGHTS

Birthday Tulips

A graceful and relatively simple appliqué pattern creates a delightfully feminine bed quilt. The delicacy of the appliqué is mirrored in the feathered quilting that fills the border and the spaces surrounding the center medallion. The angled bottom corners add a distinctive touch as the quilt drapes over the bed.

Skill Level: Intermediate

Size: Finished quilt is 90 × 113 inches
Finished block is 15 inches square

Fabrics and Supplies

- 9 yards of muslin for background of appliqué blocks, setting blocks, borders, and binding
- 2½ yards of solid dark burgundy fabric for appliqués and borders
- 2 yards of solid pink fabric for appliqués and borders
- ¾ yard of solid green fabric for stems and leaves
- ½ yard of medium pink print fabric for appliqués
- 3⅓ yards of 108-inch-wide muslin for quilt back
- King-size quilt batting (120 inches square)
- Rotary cutter, ruler, and mat
- Template plastic
- Thread to match the appliqué fabrics

Cutting

All measurements include ¼-inch seam allowances. Measurements for the borders are longer than needed; trim them to the exact length when they are added to the quilt. For the pink and burgundy borders on the sides, you will need to piece strips together.

Make templates for the large and small tulips and the tulip leaf appliqués from the patterns on page 76. Tips for making and using templates are on page 152. The large tulip has three pattern pieces (A, B, and C). The smaller one has two (D and E). The pattern pieces are given finished size; add seam allowances when you cut out the fabric. Note that the tulip colors are reversed in the inner and outer blocks; refer to the **Fabric Key** and **Diagram 1** for correct color placement. To mark reverse pieces, turn the templates over so the wrong side is facing up.

Before You Begin

To cut the muslin, first divide the yardage into one 3¼-yard (117-inch) piece and one 5¾-yard (207-inch) piece.

From the 117-inch piece of muslin, cut:
- Two 9½ × 117-inch side border strips
- One 9½ × 85-inch bottom border strip
- One 7½ × 63-inch top border strip

From the 207-inch piece of muslin, cut:
- Sixteen 15½-inch square blocks
- Four 15½ × 30½-inch rectangular setting pieces
- Reserve the remaining fabric for binding

From the solid burgundy fabric, cut:
- Four 3½ × 90-inch strips (the length of the fabric)
- 12 B pieces
- 4 C pieces
- 8 D and 8 D reverse pieces
- 24 E pieces

From the solid pink fabric, cut:
- Five 2½ × 72-inch outer border strips
- Five 1½ × 72-inch inner border strips
- 4 B pieces
- 12 C pieces
- 24 D and 24 D reverse pieces
- 8 E pieces

From the solid green fabric, cut:
- 1¼-inch-wide bias strips for stems. (Each of the 16 Tulip blocks needs two 13½-inch-long strips and one 4½-inch-long strip. Cut long strips of bias from the fabric, and cut the individual pieces from the long strips. You will need a total of 504 inches of bias strips.)
- 16 F and 16 F reverse pieces

From the medium pink print fabric, cut:
- 16 A pieces

Making the Blocks

1. Make one 4½-inch-long and two 13½-inch-long bias strips for stems in each of the 16 Tulip blocks. Refer to page 157 for instructions on making bias strips. Baste the prepared strips to the blocks, referring to the measurements on the **Block Diagram** for correct placement.

2. You will make 4 inner blocks and 12 outer blocks. Referring to **Diagram 1** and the **Block Diagram,** pin the tulip pieces in position. For each large middle tulip, stack the pieces in A-B-C order. For each smaller side tulip, position the E piece under the D and D reverse pieces. Note that for the quilt's 4 inner blocks, the fabrics are arranged as shown in **Diagram 1A;** for the 12 outer blocks, the colors are reversed, as shown in **Diagram 1B.**

3. Stitch the appliqués in place, using a blind hem stitch and threads that match the appliqué fabrics. Refer to page 156 for tips on hand appliqué.

Assembling the Quilt Top

1. Referring to the **Quilt Diagram** to position the blocks properly, join the blocks and rectangular setting pieces in horizontal rows to form the inner quilt. The top row is made up of four outer blocks, and the second row has two outer blocks with a plain rectangle between them. For the center portion of the quilt (which forms the third row), sew four inner blocks together with stems meeting; then sew setting rectangles to opposite sides. The fourth and fifth rows are reverses of the second and first. Refer to page 159 for instructions on assembling quilt tops. The assembled blocks should measure $60\frac{1}{2} \times 90\frac{1}{2}$ inches, including seam allowances.

2. Measure the top edge of the quilt and trim the $7\frac{1}{2}$-inch-wide muslin top border strip as needed. Attach the border strip and press the seam toward the border.

3. Use two of the $1\frac{1}{2} \times 72$-inch solid pink strips for the top and bottom inner borders. Cut one of the three remaining strips in half. Sew a half-strip to an end of each of the two remaining 72-inch strips to achieve the length needed for the sides. Add the borders to all four sides, mitering the corners. Refer to page 159 for instructions on adding and mitering borders. Press the seams toward the border.

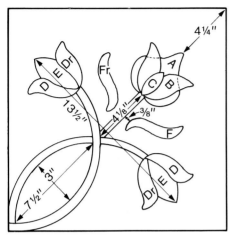

Block Diagram

Fabric Key

☐ Pink

▨ Burgundy

▨ Pink print

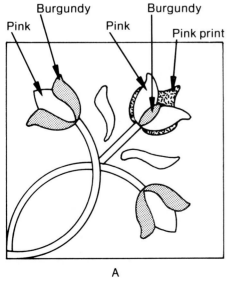

A

Inner Blocks

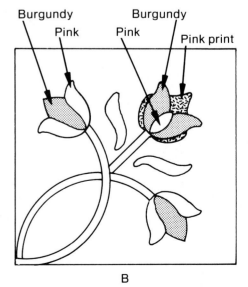

B

Outer Blocks

Diagram 1

Top

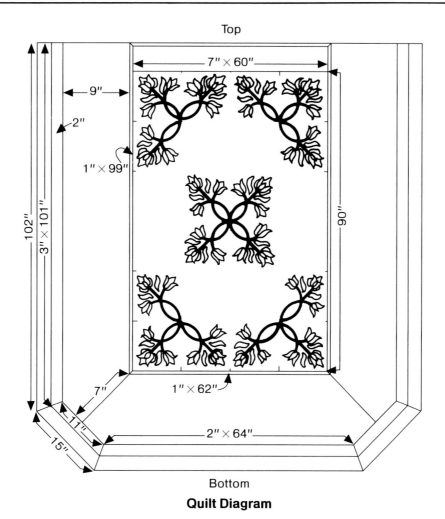

Bottom

Quilt Diagram

4. Measure, trim as needed, and add the 9½-inch-wide muslin border strips to the sides and the bottom of the quilt, mitering the two bottom corners. Press the seams toward the muslin border. At the bottom corners, measure out 7¼ inches from the solid pink border corners and trim off the muslin corner at a right angle to the miter seam, as shown in **Diagram 2.**

5. To make the solid pink and burgundy side borders, you will need to piece strips together to achieve the required length. Cut one of the 2½ × 72-inch solid pink border strips in half. Sew each half-strip to the end of an uncut 72-inch solid pink border strip. Cut two 15-inch-long pieces from one of the 3½ × 90-inch burgundy strips. Sew each 15-inch piece to the end of an uncut 90-inch burgundy strip. Sew the solid pink and burgundy side borders together. Set aside.

6. Join the 3½ × 90-inch burgundy border and the 2½ × 72-inch solid pink border to make the

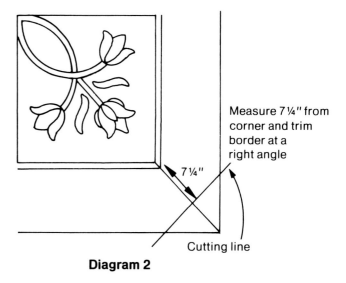

Measure 7¼" from corner and trim border at a right angle

Cutting line

Diagram 2

bottom border, trimming the excess burgundy fabric. To make the angled corner borders, sew the 3½ × 60-inch burgundy border strip left over from Step 5 to the last 2½ × 72-inch solid pink border strip, trimming the excess pink fabric. You will need a strip combination of 40 inches. From this strip, cut one 20-inch piece for each corner.

7. Sew the side borders from Step 5 to the quilt, stopping the stitching ¼ inch from the bottom edge. Sew the bottom borders to the quilt, again stopping the stitching ¼ inch from each end.

8. Attach the angled corner borders to the quilt and miter the seams. Press all the seams away from the center of the quilt.

Quilting and Finishing

1. Mark quilting designs on the completed quilt top. The quilt shown has a 1-inch diagonal grid

in the inner area of the quilt, and straight-line quilting 1 inch apart on the borders. The blocks are quilted in the ditch around all the appliqué shapes. Flowing feather motifs are quilted in the muslin rectangles and the borders.

2. Layer the backing, batting, and quilt top;

3. Quilt all marked designs.

4. Using the remaining muslin, make French-fold binding. You will need approximately 415 inches (11⅝ yards). Refer to page 164 for instructions on making and attaching binding. Sew the binding to the quilt top, turn, and hand finish on the back.

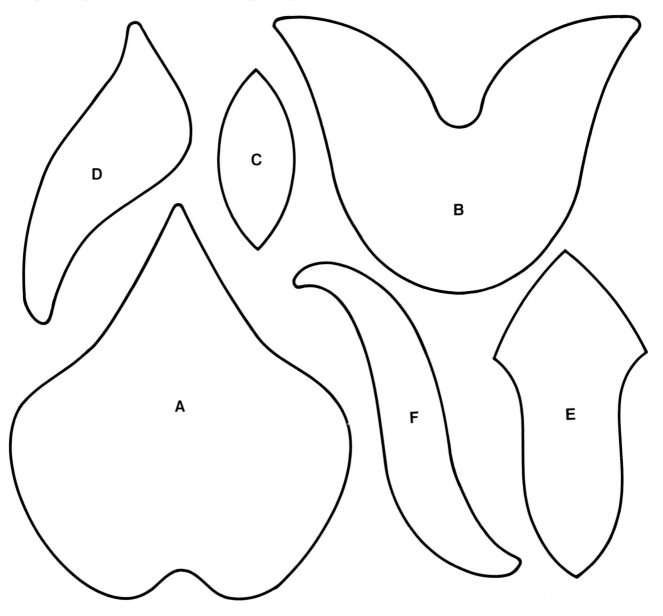

Amish Fans and Roses

Fifteen rich, jewel-tone fabrics in colors favored by Amish quiltmakers shimmer against a black background. While at first glance this quilt may seem complex, the main portion is actually made up of rows of the same fan blocks turned in different directions. Simple red and black borders frame the quilt center, and an elaborate fan border seems to dance along the edges. The "roses" in the title come from the rose quilting design.

Skill Level: Intermediate

Size: Finished quilt is 78½ × 90½ inches
Finished block is 6 inches square

Fabrics and Supplies

- 6½ yards of solid black fabric for blocks and borders
- 2¼ yards of solid red fabric for fan centers, borders, and binding
- ¾ yard *each* of 14 Amish-inspired fabrics for the fan blades. (The colors used in the quilt shown are dusty rose, rust, light aqua, teal, brown, deep coral, two shades of blue, three shades of medium purple, and three shades of green.)
- 6 yards of solid black fabric for quilt back
- Lightweight quilt batting or prewashed cotton flannel, larger than 78½ × 90½ inches
- Template plastic
- Rotary cutter, ruler, and mat
- Thread to match the appliqué fabrics

Cutting

Make templates for the fan center and the fan blade using patterns A and B on page 81. Refer to page 152 for tips on making and using templates. The patterns and all measurements include ¼-inch seam allowances. Measurements for the borders are longer than needed; trim them to the exact length later when they are added to the quilt top.

Before You Begin
To prepare the solid black fabric for piecing, first cut the 6½-yard piece into an 85-inch-long piece and a 149-inch-long piece.

From the 85-inch piece of solid black fabric, cut:
- Four 7½ × 85-inch outer border strips
- Four 1¼ × 85-inch narrow border strips

From the 149-inch piece of solid black fabric, cut:
- One hundred twenty 6½-inch squares

  Quick-Cutting Method: Cut 6½ × 44-inch strips; cut each strip into 6½-inch squares.

From the solid red fabric, cut:
- Eight 1¼ × 81-inch border strips

- 120 fan centers (**Pattern B**)
- Reserve the remaining fabric for binding

From each of the 14 assorted fabrics, cut:
- Approximately 70 fan blades (**Pattern A**). You will only need a total of 920 fan blades, but having more will allow you more choices when combining colors.

Preparing the Fan Blades

1. Fold a fan blade piece in half lengthwise with right sides facing, as shown in **Diagram 1.** Using a ¼-inch seam, stitch across the top edge of the blade. Trim the seam to ⅛ inch to reduce bulk.

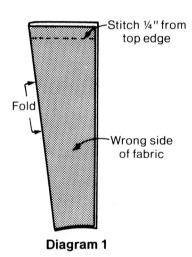

Stitch ¼″ from top edge

Fold

Wrong side of fabric

Diagram 1

2. Turn the stitched section right-side out and center the seam along the wrong side of the blade, as shown in **Diagram 2.** Press well. Prepare each of the fan blades in this manner.

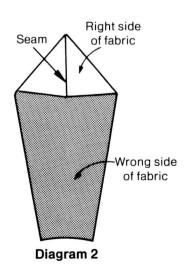

Seam

Right side of fabric

Wrong side of fabric

Diagram 2

Making the Fan Blocks

1. Make 120 fan blocks. For each block, you will need five assorted blades, one fan center, and one black background square.

2. Turn under ¼ inch on the curved edge of the fan center piece and baste. Referring to the **Block Diagram,** pin the fan center to one corner of the background square.

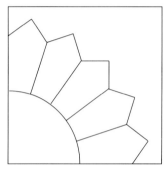

Block Diagram

3. Sew together five fan blades. Press the seams in one direction. Pin the fan to the background square, slipping the curved bottom edge of the fan ¼ inch under the curved basted edge of the center.

4. Appliqué the curved edge of the fan center to the fan blades. Appliqué the pointed edges of the blades to the background square. See page 156 for tips on appliqué.

5. Baste the sides of the fan and the fan center to the background square in the seam allowance.

Assembling the Quilt Top

1. Referring to the **Quilt Diagram,** lay out the fan blocks in 12 horizontal rows with 10 blocks in each row. The four center blocks form a circle, and the remaining fans form rings around the center circle.

2. Stitch the blocks together in rows, pressing the seams in alternate directions from row to row. Join the rows. Refer to page 159 for instructions on

90½"

78½"

Quilt Diagram

assembling quilt tops. If you plan to add quilting to the fan portion of the blocks, as this quiltmaker did, you will need to trim away the fabric behind the applique. Refer to "Trimming from behind Appliqués" on page 91 for tips.

3. Measure the length of the quilt top. Trim two red border strips to this length and sew them to the sides of the quilt top. Press the seams toward the borders. Measure the width of the quilt top, including the red borders. Trim two red border strips to this length and sew them to the top and bottom of the quilt top. Press the seams toward the borders.

4. In the same manner, continue to measure and trim border strips to length before adding them to the quilt top. Add the 1¼-inch black border strips to the quilt, then add the other set of red border strips.

5. Measure, trim, and add the 7½-inch black border strips to the sides of the quilt and then to the top and bottom.

Adding the Fan Borders

1. Make 64 five-blade units. To make one unit, sew together five assorted fan blades. Press the seam allowances in one direction. Turn under the seam allowance along the bottom curved edge of the unit and baste.

2. Referring to the **Quilt Diagram** and **Diagram 3** for correct placement, sew together 13 five-blade units for the top border and 13 units for the bottom border. Alternate the direction of the fans as shown, and begin and end each border with units that have blades pointing toward the quilt center.

3. In a similar manner, sew together 15 units for each side border.

4. Make four ten-blade corner units by sewing together pairs of five-blade units so they form half-circles. Turn under the seam allowance along the bottom curved edge of the corner units and baste.

5. Referring to the **Quilt Diagram** and **Diagram 3,** pin the five-blade units to the wide black borders on the sides and ends of the quilt. Pin the corner units in position, adding or taking off blades as needed to make the borders fit your quilt. When you've adjusted the fit, pin all the borders securely in place. Stitch the corner units to the five-blade units using a blind stitch.

6. Appliqué the fan borders to the black borders.

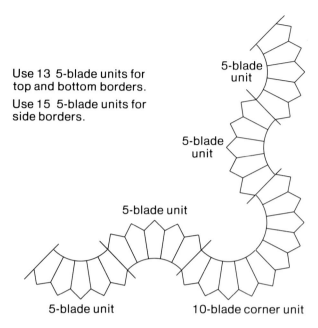

Use 13 5-blade units for top and bottom borders.

Use 15 5-blade units for side borders.

5-blade unit

5-blade unit

5-blade unit

5-blade unit

10-blade corner unit

Diagram 3

Quilting and Finishing

1. Mark the **Rosebud Quilting Design** on the opposite page onto each blade. Mark the **Rose Quilting Design** also on the opposite page in the black background areas, adding additional leaves as desired to fill the spaces. On the fan center pieces, extend the lines from the rosebud stems into the block corner and draw a line into the corner from the seams joining the blades, as shown in **Diagram 4.**

Diagram 4

2. Cut the 6 yards of backing fabric in half across the width and trim the selvages. Cut one of the 3-yard pieces in half lengthwise, and sew one half to each long side of the other 3-yard piece. If you are using flannel instead of batting, you may need to piece the flannel to accommodate the quilt top. Layer the quilt back, batting or flannel, and quilt top; baste.

3. Outline quilt around all the fan pieces and borders, and quilt all the marked designs, adding additional quilting as desired.

4. Cut French-fold binding from the remaining red fabric. Refer to page 164 for suggested binding widths and instructions on making and attaching binding. You will need approximately 355 inches (9⅞ yards) of binding. Piece the binding into two strips approximately 2 inches longer than the quilt sides, and two strips approximately 2 inches longer than the quilt top and bottom.

5. Sew the binding to the sides of the quilt. Turn the binding to the quilt back and hand stitch it in place; trim the ends of the binding even with the edges of the quilt.

6. Sew the binding to the top and bottom of the quilt, allowing at least ¼ inch extra binding at each end. Turn under the raw ends of the binding so that they are even with the edge of the quilt. Turn the binding to the quilt back and stitch in place, adding extra stitches to secure the ends of the binding.

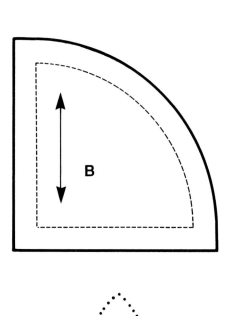

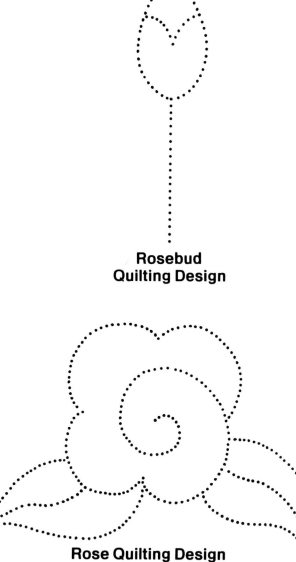

**Rosebud
Quilting Design**

Rose Quilting Design

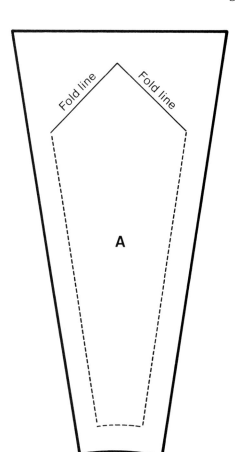

A Walk in the Park

Pretty prints combine with muslin in this classic Boston Commons quilt. The four blue and two pink prints used are similar in shade, but have contrast in scale (size of print) and value (dark versus light). This contrast helps define the pattern. Quick-cutting and strip-piecing are ideal modern techniques that speed up making this traditional beauty.

Skill Level: Intermediate

Size: Finished quilt is 90 × 105 inches

Fabrics and Supplies

- 5¼ yards of Fabric 1 (muslin) for patchwork and borders
- 1¼ yards *each* of the following five fabrics for patchwork:

    Fabric 2 (blue print)
    Fabric 3 (blue print)
    Fabric 4 (blue print)
    Fabric 5 (blue print)
    Fabric 6 (pink print)

- 1½ yards of Fabric 7 (pink print) for patchwork and binding
- 3¼ yards of 108-inch-wide fabric for quilt back
- King-size quilt batting (120 inches square)
- Rotary cutter, ruler, and mat

Cutting

All measurements for strips and borders include ¼-inch seam allowances. Measurements for the borders are longer than needed; trim them to the exact length when they are added to the quilt top.

From the muslin, cut:
- Sixteen 2¼ × 44-inch strips
- Two 8 × 111-inch side outer border strips and two 8 × 96-inch top and bottom outer border strips
- Two 8 × 65-inch side inner border strips and two 8 × 51-inch top and bottom inner border strips

From each of Fabrics 2 through 6, cut:
- Sixteen 2¼ × 44-inch strips

From Fabric 7, cut:
- Eight 2¼ × 44-inch strips
- Reserve the remaining fabric for binding

Before You Begin

The method described for making this quilt involves constructing a specific strip set and then cutting that set into narrow strips of joined squares. You will take apart some of the short seams that join the squares to make the shorter rows needed to construct the sections of the quilt.

The quilt is made of four kinds of sections: Corner Sections (six total), Side Sections (two total), End Sections (two total), and one Center Section. One type of partial section, labeled T in the instructions, is used in all but the Center Section of the quilt.

Making Strip Sets

1. Referring to **Diagram 1** and the **Fabric Key,** and using ¼-inch seam allowances, sew 13 strips into a strip set. To make each set, you will need two strips each of Fabrics 1 through 6, and one of Fabric 7. Sew the strips in the order shown and press all the seams in one direction. Repeat to make a total of eight identical sets.

Fabric Key

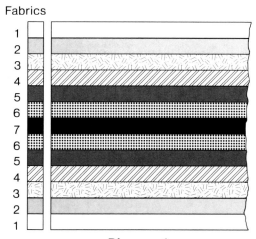

□ 1 (muslin)

▨ 2 (blue print)

▨ 3 (blue print)

▨ 4 (blue print)

■ 5 (blue print)

▦ 6 (pink print)

■ 7 (pink print)

Diagram 1

2. Cut the eight strip sets into 2¼-inch-wide strips, as shown in **Diagram 1.** You should get 18 to 19 strips per set. You will need a total of 144 strips. These strips are labeled S on the diagrams.

Making Triangular T Units

Construct 16 triangular T Units to use in making the various quilt sections. These T Units are used in all but the Center Section of the quilt. To make one T Unit:

1. Use six S Strips to create the 12 rows of strips in the unit. Start by making Rows 6 and 7. To make those rows, take apart one seam of an S Strip so that you have a partial strip with six squares and a partial strip with seven squares, as shown in **Diagram 2.** Position the two rows as shown in **Diagram 3,** with the shorter row on the bottom. Join the rows.

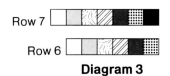

Diagram 2

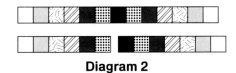

Diagram 3

2. To make Rows 5 and 8, take apart an S Strip to create a partial strip with five squares and one with eight squares. Sew the Row 5 strip to Row 6 and the Row 8 strip to Row 7, as shown in **Diagram 4.**

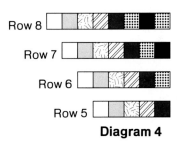

Diagram 4

3. Continue separating the S Strips and adding them to the previously joined rows to create the 12-row triangular T Unit. Your completed unit should look like the one in **Diagram 5.** You will use six strips to create each T Unit.

Triangular T Unit

Piecing Diagram

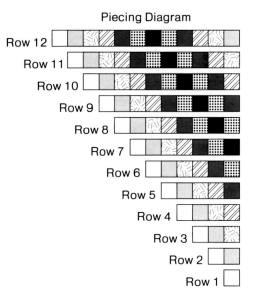

Completed Unit

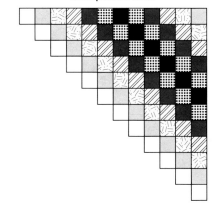

Diagram 5

Assembling the Quilt Sections

The quilt sections consist of T Units combined with S Strips.

Corner Sections

Use one S Strip. Sew a T Unit to each side of the strip, offsetting the strip by one square, as shown in **Diagram 6.** Make six Corner Sections.

Corner Section

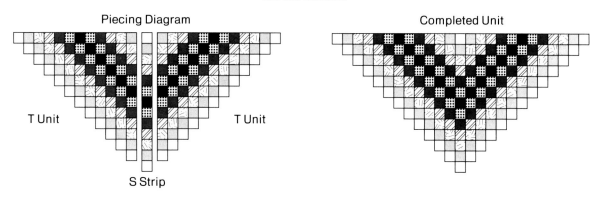

Diagram 6

Side Sections

1. Join 11 S Strips, offsetting each by one square, as shown in **Diagram 7.**

2. Sew a T Unit to the 11-strip section, as shown. Make two Side Sections.

Side Section

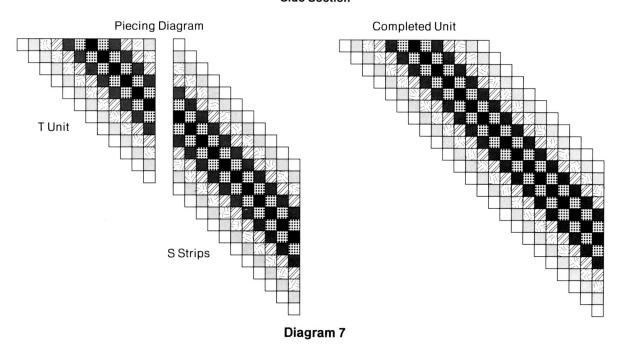

Diagram 7

End Sections

1. Join five S Strips, offsetting each by one square, as shown in **Diagram 8.**

2. Sew a T Unit to the five-strip unit, as shown. Make two End Sections.

End Section

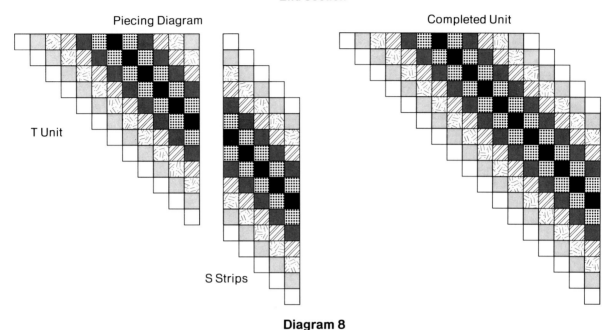

Piecing Diagram

Completed Unit

T Unit

S Strips

Diagram 8

Center Section

1. Use ten S Strips. Remove the Fabric 1 square from one end of five of the strips to make partial strips.

2. Join a partial strip and a full-length strip to make a long strip with a Fabric 1 square at each end and one in the middle, as shown in **Diagram 9.** Make a total of five long strips.

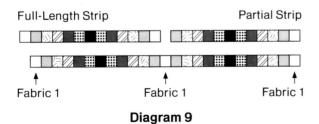

Full-Length Strip   Partial Strip

Fabric 1   Fabric 1   Fabric 1

Diagram 9

3. Join the five long strips, offsetting each strip by one block, to complete the Center Section. See **Diagram 10.** You will need only one Center Section.

Center Section

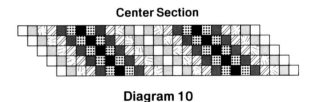

Diagram 10

Assembling the Quilt Top

1. Referring to **Diagram 11,** join the Center Section and two Corner Sections to make the pieced inner quilt.

2. Before adding the inner borders, use a ruler and pencil to make a small dot on the muslin square

Piecing Diagram   Completed Unit

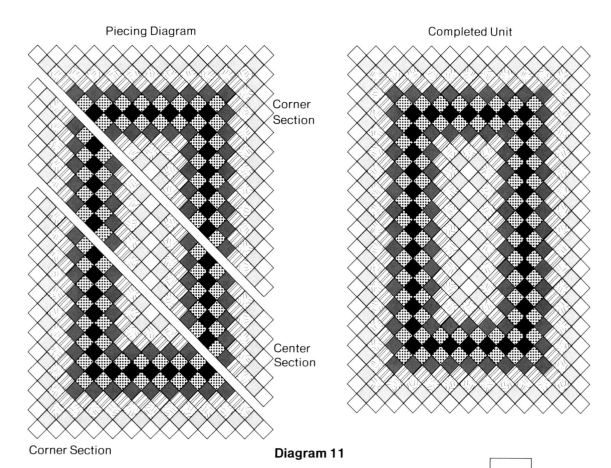

Corner
Section

Center
Section

Corner Section   **Diagram 11**

at each of the four corners of the quilt top. Align the ruler with the inside of the Vs created along two edges of the inner quilt, and make a dot where the two lines intersect, as shown in **Diagram 12.**

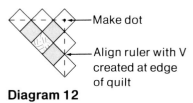

Make dot

Align ruler with V
created at edge
of quilt

Diagram 12

3. Fold a side border strip in half, short ends together, to find the center. Fold the quilt top in half, short ends together, to find the center. Place the border strip, right sides together, with the quilt top, matching the centers. Line up the edge of the border strip with the inside of the Vs created along the edge of the quilt top, and leave the uneven edges of the muslin squares extended, as shown in **Diagram 13.** Attach the border strip, stitching between the pencil dots only. Press the seam allowance toward the border.

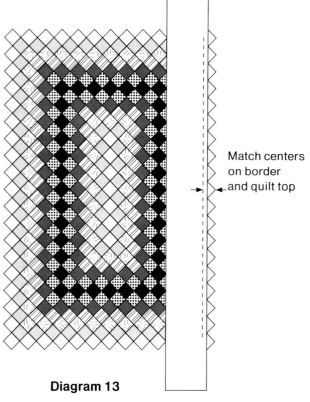

Match centers
on border
and quilt top

Diagram 13

4. Attach all four border strips and miter the corners. Refer to page 159 for instructions on adding and mitering borders. After you have attached all four borders and mitered the corners, trim off the extended muslin triangles. The quilt top, with the muslin borders added, should measure approximately $45\frac{1}{2} \times 60\frac{1}{2}$ inches, including seam allowances.

5. Referring to the **Quilt Diagram,** center and sew Side and End Sections to the quilt top, letting the uneven edges of the muslin outer squares extend as before. Press the seams toward the inner border. Trim off the extended triangles after sewing.

6. Sew the four remaining Corner Sections to the four corners of the quilt top, centering them on the diagonal miter seams of the inner muslin borders, as shown in the **Quilt Diagram.**

7. Add the outer border strips and miter the corners as described in Steps 2 through 4 above. Press the seams toward the borders. The quilt top, with borders added, should measure approximately $90\frac{1}{2} \times 105\frac{1}{2}$ inches, including seam allowances.

Quilting and Finishing

1. Mark quilting designs on the completed quilt top. The quilt shown has straight-line quilting through the diagonals of the patchwork squares and small diagonal background grids in the two muslin borders. The inner border has a feather motif and the outer border contains a cable design.

2. Layer the backing, batting, and quilt top; baste. Quilt all marked designs.

3. Use the remaining Fabric 7 yardage to make French-fold binding. See page 164 for instructions on making and attaching binding. You will need approximately 400 inches ($10\frac{1}{2}$ yards) of binding.

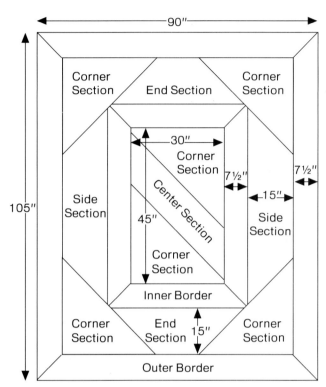

Quilt Diagram

Princess Feather
and Rose of Sharon

Unusual color choices set this unique quilt apart from standard versions of this classic pattern. Four large Princess Feather blocks, with a central Rose of Sharon appliqué, work together beautifully. Stylized flower shapes and whimsical stars sprinkled in the border give the quilt an almost folk-art character.

Skill Level: Challenging

Size: Finished quilt is 82 inches square
Finished block is 33 inches square

Fabrics and Supplies

- 5½ yards of solid green fabric for appliqués, borders, and binding
- 5 yards of solid khaki fabric for blocks and border appliqués
- 1 yard of deep rose print fabric for appliqués and unfilled piping border
- ¼ yard of light pink print fabric for appliqués
- ¼ yard of solid yellow fabric for appliqués
- 2½ yards of 90-inch-wide fabric for quilt back
- Queen-size quilt batting (90 × 108 inches)
- Rotary cutter, ruler, and mat
- Template plastic
- Thread to match the appliqué fabrics

Cutting

The cutting dimensions for borders include ¼-inch seam allowances for the widths and several extra inches in length; trim the borders to the exact length when they are added to the quilt top. The dimensions for the large background squares include an extra 1½ inches; trim the blocks to the correct size after the appliqué is complete. The patterns for the appliqués are given finished size on pages 93–96. Tips on making and using templates are on page 152. Add seam allowances when cutting the pieces from the fabric. Due to its size, the large feather appliqué pattern is given in two pieces; trace each piece and join them together as indicated.

From the solid green fabric, cut:
- Two 8½ × 86-inch top and bottom border strips and two 8½ × 70-inch side border strips
- 32 large feather appliqués
- 4 long bud stem appliqués
- 4 short bud stem appliqués
- 8 double-leaf units
- Reserve the remaining fabric for binding

From the solid khaki fabric, cut:
- Four 35-inch background squares
- 28 small border feather appliqués
- 24 border stars

From the deep rose print fabric, cut:
- Seven 1 × 44-inch strips
- 5 large flowers
- 8 bud tips

From the light pink print fabric, cut:
- 5 small flowers

From the solid yellow fabric, cut:
- 5 flower centers

Making the Princess Feather Blocks

1. Fold a 35-inch khaki square in half vertically, horizontally, and diagonally both ways, and press lightly to form positioning lines.

2. Referring to the **Feather Appliqué Placement Diagram,** appliqué the eight large feather pieces first. Refer to page 157 for instructions on needle-turn appliqué. Place the stem bases approximately 3 inches from the center of the block. Be sure to place the stems so that the raw ends will be covered by the large flower when it is added at the center. To help position the feather correctly, place the template you used to make the appliqué piece over the appliqué piece and align the placement guidelines on the template with the positioning lines you pressed into the background fabric. Use matching thread to stitch the appliqué. See "Trimming from behind Appliqués" on the opposite page for tips on cutting away the background fabric after adding the appliqués.

Feather Appliqué Placement Diagram

TRIMMING FROM BEHIND APPLIQUÉS

Background fabric should be trimmed away from behind appliqué pieces when elements are stacked on top of one another, such as the flower appliqués in this Princess Feather and Rose of Sharon quilt. Trimming away the excess fabric will keep the quilt top from becoming thick and bulky. The background should also be trimmed away when quilting is planned on an appliqué piece, such as on the appliqué feathers in this quilt or on the fan blades of the Amish Fans and Roses quilt (page 77). Quilting will be easier without an extra layer of fabric. And, if the fabric underneath is darker than the appliqué, trimming will prevent the background from showing through.

To trim, turn the block or quilt top wrong-side up and work from the back. Pinch the background or underlying fabric and gently separate it from the appliqué piece. Make a small cut in the background fabric and then insert the scissors in the hole. Cut a scant ¼ inch to the inside of the line of appliqué stitches, as shown in **Diagram 1**. ◆

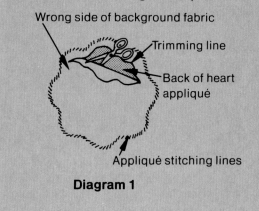

Diagram 1

2. Referring to the photograph and the **Rose of Sharon Appliqué Placement Diagram** for accurate placement, position and appliqué the Rose of Sharon pieces in the center of the quilt. Use the seams that join the four blocks as positioning guidelines. Appliqué the pieces in this order: bud tips, leaf units, long stems, short stems, large flower, small flower, flower center. The bud tips of the long stems are approximately 10 inches from the center of the quilt. The bud tips of the short stems are approximately 6 inches from the center.

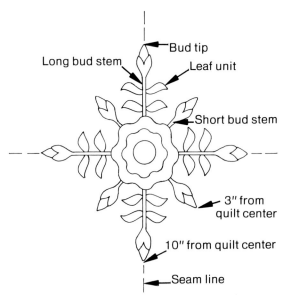

Rose of Sharon Appliqué Placement Diagram

Appliquéing the Borders

These instructions are for appliquéing in the traditional manner. The borders on the quilt shown were actually reverse appliquéd. If you wish to try your hand at reverse appliqué, refer to "Reverse Appliqué for Border Motifs" on page 92.

1. Measure the inner quilt top. It should be approximately 66½ inches square, including seam allowances. Using your measurement, mark sewing and cutting lines on the ends of the wrong side of the two 8½ × 70-inch side border strips. Wait to trim until after the appliqué is complete.

Add 16 inches to the measurement you just marked on the 70-inch side border strips, and mark sewing and cutting lines on the wrong side of the two 8½ × 86-inch top and bottom border strips. Wait to trim.

2. Referring to the photograph for placement, appliqué three pairs of small feathers and five stars

3. Center and appliqué the large flower so that it covers the ends of the stems. Add the small flower and then the flower center.

4. Measure and trim the completed blocks to 33½ inches square.

Adding the Rose of Sharon

1. Sew together the four completed Princess Feather blocks in two rows of two blocks per row. Refer to page 159 for instructions on assembling quilt tops.

REVERSE APPLIQUÉ FOR BORDER MOTIFS

Reverse appliqué is a technique in which a top fabric is cut and turned back to reveal another fabric underneath. The feather motifs in the border of the Princess Feather and Rose of Sharon quilt can be treated as regular appliqués, or they can be worked in reverse appliqué as described here.

1. Make freezer paper patterns for the border feather and star.

2. Referring to the photograph for placement, position and press the templates onto the green border strips. Lightly mark placement lines along the edges of the patterns, then remove the patterns.

3. Use the patterns to cut out the khaki rectangles (for the feathers) and squares (for the stars). Make these 1 inch larger on all four sides than the appliqués.

4. Using a light box or window, position and pin the khaki fabric pieces beneath the marked placement lines, making sure there is adequate margin all the way around the lines. Carefully cut out the top fabric, cutting approximately $3/16$ inch *to the inside of the marked lines* and taking care not to cut into the underneath fabric.

5. Carefully clip concave curves and indentations. Use thread that matches the top fabric and an appliqué needle to turn under the raw edges and stitch in place. ◆

to each side border. Appliqué four pairs of small feathers and seven stars to the top and bottom borders. Check the lengths of your completed borders with the quilt top; trim off excess border strips along the marked cutting line.

Assembling the Quilt Top

1. To make the unfilled piping border that appears between the inner quilt and the appliquéd border, piece together the seven 1-inch-wide rose strips, joining them with straight seams. Press the seams open. Press the long strip in half lengthwise, with wrong sides together. Cut the pressed strip into four 68-inch lengths of piping.

2. Place a length of piping along one side of the quilt, aligning the raw edges of the piping with the raw edges of the quilt top, and pin in place.

3. Place a completed side border, right sides together, with the piping, and sew the border to the quilt, sewing in the piping at the same time. Press the seams toward the border. Trim the excess piping from the ends after sewing.

4. In the same manner, sew piping and a side border to the opposite side of the quilt top. Then add the remaining piping strips and borders to the top and bottom of the quilt top. The completed top should measure approximately 82½ inches square, including seam allowances.

Quilting and Finishing

1. Mark quilting designs. The quilting designs for the feathers and the star appliqués are printed within the appliqué patterns on pages 94–96. Refer to the photograph to determine the correct placement of the other quilting designs. The spaces at the ends of the long bud stem appliqués, the center of the four sides, and the inner corners of the quilt have additional feather designs. A 1-inch diagonal grid fills the rest of the inner quilt.

2. Layer the backing, batting, and quilt top; baste.

3. Quilt all marked designs. In addition to the quilting designs described above, the quilt shown has outline quilting in the ditch around all the appliqués. The border motifs are echo quilted. See page 160 for more information on echo quilting.

4. Make French-fold binding from the remaining green fabric. You will need approximately 335 inches (9⅜ yards) of binding. Refer to page 164 for instructions on making and attaching binding. Sew the binding to the quilt.

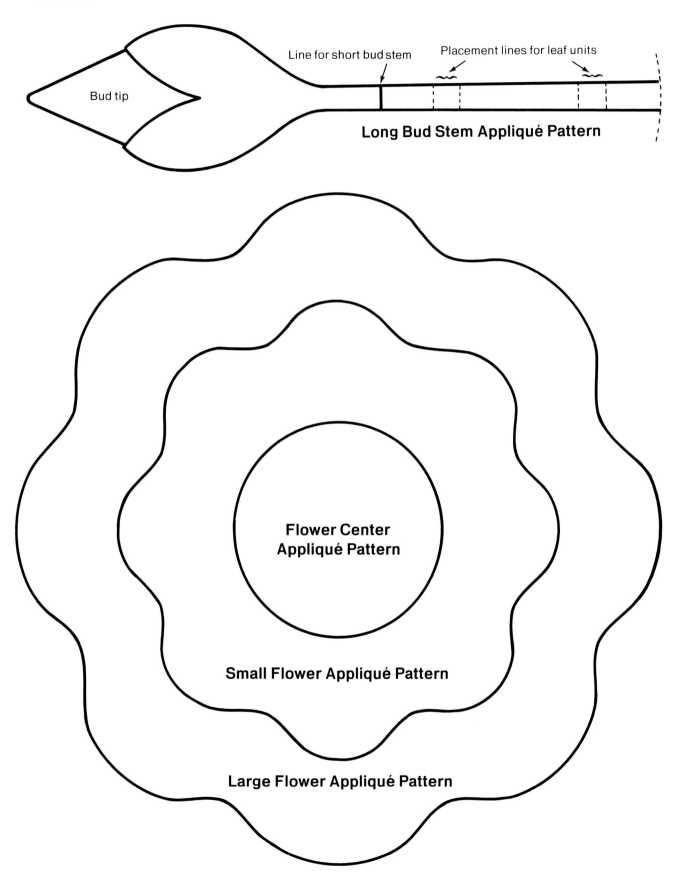

Bud tip

Line for short bud stem

Placement lines for leaf units

Long Bud Stem Appliqué Pattern

**Flower Center
Appliqué Pattern**

Small Flower Appliqué Pattern

Large Flower Appliqué Pattern

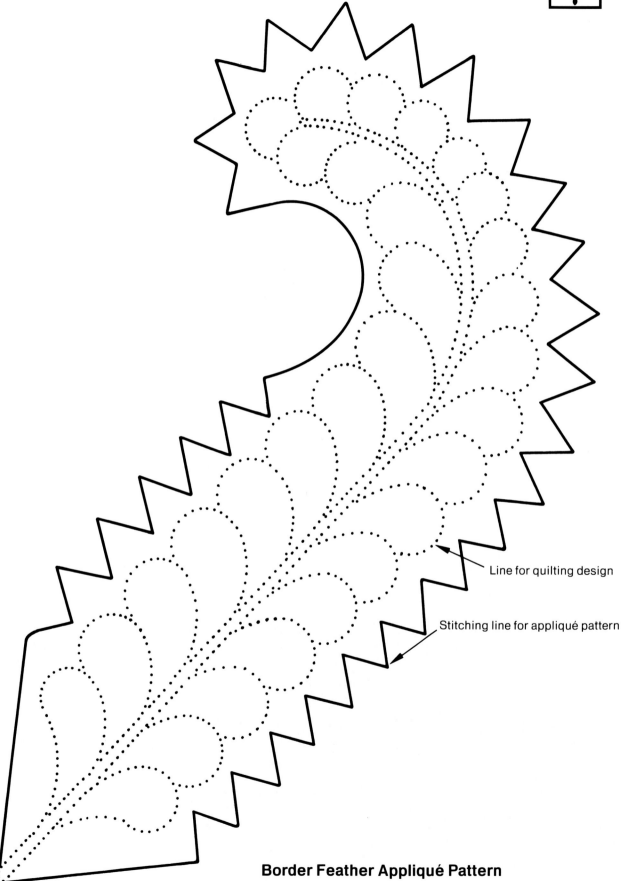

Line for quilting design

Stitching line for appliqué pattern

Border Feather Appliqué Pattern

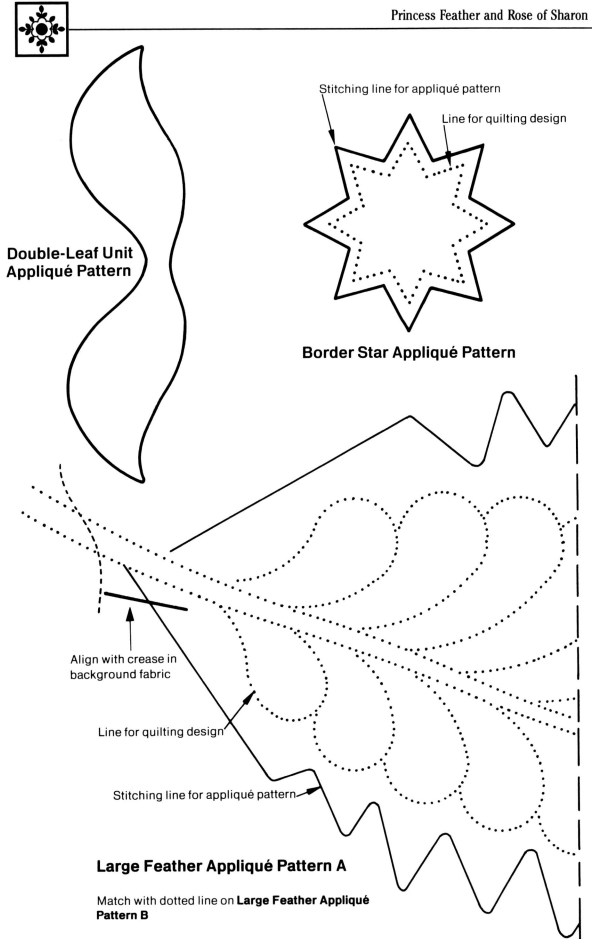

Double-Leaf Unit Appliqué Pattern

Stitching line for appliqué pattern

Line for quilting design

Border Star Appliqué Pattern

Align with crease in background fabric

Line for quilting design

Stitching line for appliqué pattern

Large Feather Appliqué Pattern A

Match with dotted line on **Large Feather Appliqué Pattern B**

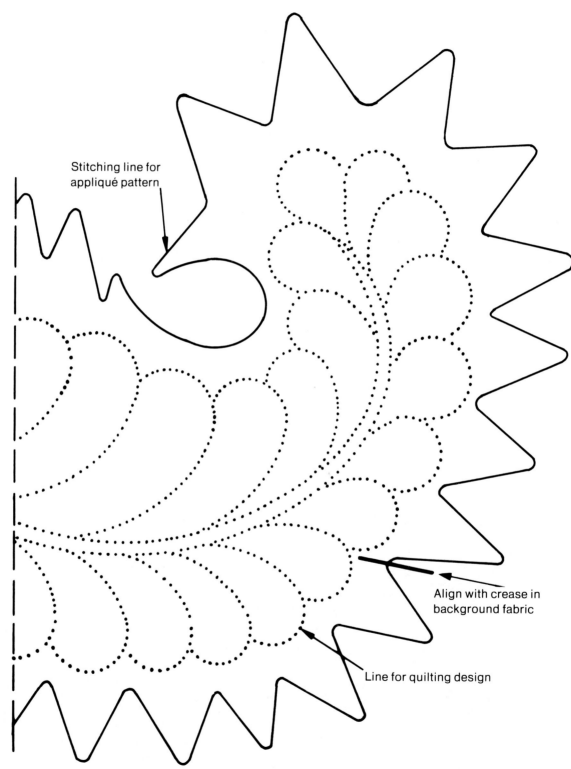

Stitching line for appliqué pattern

Align with crease in background fabric

Line for quilting design

Large Feather Appliqué Pattern B

Match with dotted line on Large Feather Appliqué Pattern A

Spring Garden

The colorful exuberance of a flower garden is captured in this quilt, which combines the LeMoyne Star block with pieced setting blocks. A creative use of fabric contributes to the quilt's unique character. Although it appears as if each block were made from a different print, the same floral fabric was used for all of the stars and for the centers of the setting blocks and triangles. A clever but simple cutting technique creates this wonderful effect.

Skill Level: Intermediate

Size: Finished quilt is 67¼ × 95½ inches
Finished block is 10 inches square

Fabrics and Supplies

- 5 yards of green print fabric for blocks, borders, and binding
- 3½ yards of cream print fabric for blocks and borders
- Approximately 3 yards of print fabric with a variety of widely spaced floral motifs for blocks. Drapery and decorator stores are good sources for floral fabrics of this type. (You will only need 1¾ yards of fabric if you do not plan to cut the fabric to achieve special effects.)
- 6 yards of fabric for quilt back
- Queen-size quilt batting (90 × 108 inches)
- Rotary cutter, ruler, and mat
- Template plastic

Cutting

All template patterns and measurements include ¼-inch seam allowances. Measurements for the borders are longer than needed; trim them to the exact length as they are added to the quilt top.

Prepare plastic templates for A, B, and C using the patterns on pages 102 and 103. Instructions for making and using templates are on page 152. Use a large needle to pierce holes through the A, B, and C templates at the points marked with dots on the patterns. As you mark each fabric piece for cutting, mark through each hole to make a dot on the fabric, indicating the beginning and ending points of seams. Quick-cutting directions are provided for the D and E pieces. If you prefer to cut these pieces in a traditional manner, make the following templates (measurements include ¼-inch seam allowances):

- **D:** Make a 5⅞-inch square; cut the square in half diagonally.
- **E:** Make a 4⅛-inch square; cut the square in half diagonally.

From the green print fabric, cut:
- Two 5 × 100-inch side outer border strips and two 5 × 75-inch top and bottom border strips

- Two 2½ × 100-inch side inner border strips and two 2½ × 75-inch top and bottom inner border strips
- 60 B triangles
- 60 C squares
- 60 E triangles

  Quick-Cutting Method: Cut three 4⅛ × 44-inch strips. From these strips, cut thirty 4⅛-inch squares. Cut each square in half diagonally to make two triangles.

- Reserve the remaining fabric for binding

From the cream print fabric, cut:
- Two 6½ × 100-inch side middle border strips and two 6½ × 75-inch top and bottom middle border strips
- 44 D triangles

  Quick-Cutting Method: Cut four 5⅞ × 44-inch strips. From these strips, cut twenty-two 5⅞-inch squares. Cut each square in half diagonally to make two triangles.

- 32 E triangles

  Quick-Cutting Method: Cut two 4⅛ × 44-inch strips. From these strips, cut sixteen 4⅛-inch squares. Cut each square in half diagonally to make two triangles.

From the floral print fabric, cut:
- 120 A diamonds. (To cut the pieces selectively to create special flowerlike designs within the quilt blocks, see "Cutting Fabrics to Create Special Effects" on the opposite page.)
- 60 E triangles

  Quick-Cutting Method: Cut three 4⅛ × 44-inch strips. From these strips, cut thirty 4⅛-inch squares. Cut each square in half diagonally to make two triangles.

Piecing the Blocks

This quilt is made up of 15 LeMoyne Star blocks and 8 pieced setting blocks. The edges are filled in with 12 half-block pieced setting triangles and 4 quarter-block pieced corner triangles.

LeMoyne Star Blocks
1. Referring to the **Fabric Key** and the **LeMoyne Star Block Diagram,** make 15 LeMoyne Star blocks. To make each block you will need four green B triangles, four green C squares, and a group of eight identical floral A diamonds. The assembly of this

block involves setting pieces into seams. As you join the pieces, sew only from dot to dot, leaving the seam allowances at the ends of the seams unstitched. See page 155 for tips on setting-in pieces.

Fabric Key

 Green

 Cream

 Floral

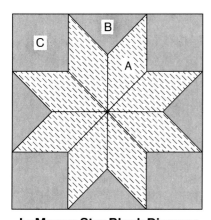

LeMoyne Star Block Diagram

Sew together four pairs of floral A diamonds, as shown in **Diagram 1.** Join the pairs into half-stars; join the halves. Press all the seam allowances to one side in a clockwise direction.

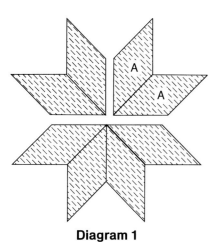

Diagram 1

CUTTING FABRICS TO CREATE SPECIAL EFFECTS

The fabric pieces for the LeMoyne Stars and the centers of the setting blocks in this Spring Garden quilt were cut from a single fabric. The fabric, patterned with a variety of widely spaced floral motifs, lets each star and setting block look uniquely different. To achieve this special effect, cut the eight diamonds for a star, or the triangles for a setting block, with the template on the same portion of the floral motif for each one.

1. Begin by making a transparent or semitransparent plastic template for the pattern piece. Choose template plastic that is easy to see through and also easy to write on with a pen or pencil.

2. To help visualize the effect you will achieve by cutting a particular fabric piece, you can use two small mirrors, approximately 3 to 4 inches square. Small, inexpensive mirrors are available in some quilt shops or in the cosmetics department of variety or discount stores.

Position the template atop the right side of the printed fabric. Set the mirrors on the template so they form a corner at the point of the template and the mirror edges are aligned with the seam lines on the template. By looking at the mirrors and the template, you will see how three repeats of the fabric pattern will look when joined together.

3. When you have a visual effect that pleases you, draw around the template. Then, with the template still in place on the fabric, trace the outline of a prominent flower or other shape from the material onto the template to help you align the template in the same position on the next pattern repeat. Cut out the fabric piece.

4. To mark successive pieces, position the template in the same relative position on the printed fabric. The design outline you drew on the template will help you align the template accurately. Make new templates when used ones become too messy to use accurately. ◆

2. Set a green B triangle into alternate openings around the star, as shown in **Diagram 2.** Press the seam allowances toward the B triangles.

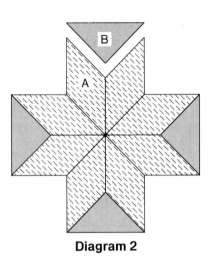

Diagram 2

3. Set a green C square into each corner opening, as shown in **Diagram 3.** Press the seam allowances toward the squares.

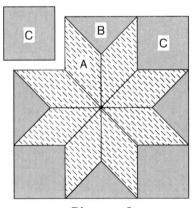

Diagram 3

Setting Blocks

1. Referring to the **Fabric Key** and the **Setting Block Diagram,** make eight setting blocks. For each block you will need four cream D triangles, four green E triangles, and a set of four matching floral E triangles.

Sew together a green E triangle and a floral E triangle to make a square. Make a total of four squares. Placing the green triangles toward the outside, join the squares into pairs, then join the pairs into a larger square, as shown in **Diagram 4.** To help create a precise center point, press the seams joining the pairs in opposite directions.

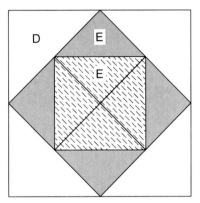

Setting Block Diagram

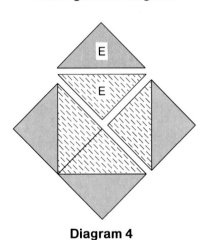

Diagram 4

2. Referring to **Diagram 5,** sew a cream D triangle to opposite sides of the larger square. Press the seam allowances toward the D triangles as you assemble the block. Sew a cream D triangle to the remaining two sides.

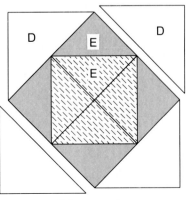

Diagram 5

Setting Triangles

1. Referring to the **Fabric Key** and the **Setting Triangle Diagram,** make 12 setting triangles. For each triangle you will need one cream D triangle, two cream E triangles, two green E triangles, and two matching floral E triangles.

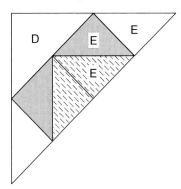

Setting Triangle Diagram

Piece two squares by joining a green E triangle to a floral E triangle. Join the squares into a rectangle with the floral triangles positioned so they form a larger triangle, as shown in **Diagram 6.** Sew the long side of a D triangle to the long green side of the rectangle.

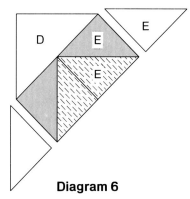

Diagram 6

2. Sew a cream E triangle to each short side of the rectangle to form a pieced triangle.

Corner Triangles

1. Referring to the **Fabric Key** and the **Corner Triangle Diagram,** make four corner triangles. For each triangle you will need one floral E triangle, one

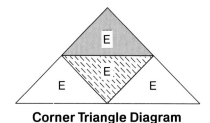

Corner Triangle Diagram

green E triangle, and two cream E triangles. Join a floral triangle to a green triangle to make a square.

2. Sew the short sides of the cream E triangles to the sides of the green E triangle to form a pieced triangle, as shown in **Diagram 7.**

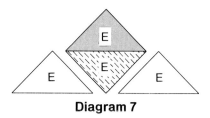

Diagram 7

Assembling the Quilt Top

1. Referring to the **Quilt Diagram** and the photograph for correct positioning, lay out the star and setting blocks in seven diagonal rows. Add a corner triangle at each corner and setting triangles in the openings around the perimeter of the quilt. When you are satisfied with the arrangement of the blocks, sew the pieces together in diagonal rows, pressing the seams in alternate directions from row to row. Join the rows. General instructions for assembling quilt tops are on page 159.

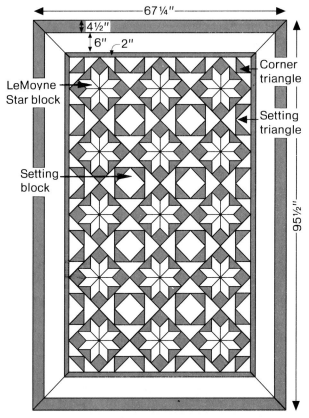

Quilt Diagram

2. To make the borders, sew together the 2½-inch green print inner border strips, the 6½-inch cream print middle border strips, and the 5-inch green print outer border strips along the long sides. Stitch two long (100-inch) borders for the sides of the quilt and two shorter (75-inch) borders for the top and bottom.

3. Sew the borders to the quilt, mitering the corners. See page 159 for instructions on adding and mitering borders.

Quilting and Finishing

1. Mark quilting designs onto the quilt top with a pencil or other removable marker. The quilt shown has outline quilting around the pieces in the blocks, plus additional lines for more interest. The borders are quilted with a cable design.

2. To piece the quilt back, divide the 6 yards of backing fabric in half, creating two 3-yard pieces. Divide one of those pieces in half lengthwise to make two 22 × 108-inch panels. Sew one of these panels to each long side of the uncut 3-yard piece. Layer the back, batting, and quilt top; baste.

3. Quilt along all marked lines, adding additional quilting as desired.

4. Cut 2-inch-wide strips from the remaining green fabric to make French-fold binding. You will need approximately 360 inches (10 yards) of binding. Sew the binding to the quilt, mitering the corners. See page 164 for instructions on making and attaching binding.

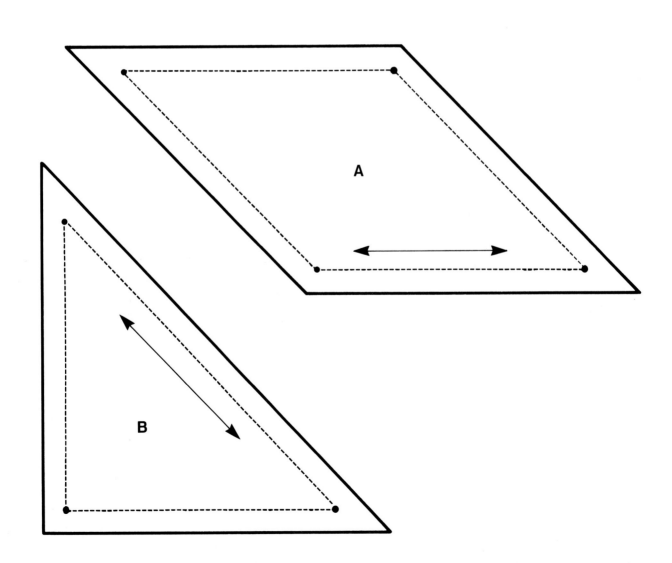

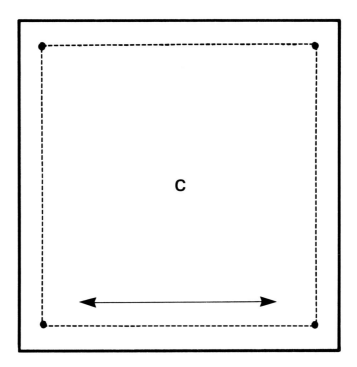

Silverainbow

A rainbow of 32 colors combined with gray creates a simple but striking quilt. Although there are 32 rows containing over 1,000 triangles, quick-cutting directions make preparing the pieces much less of a chore. Hand quilting along the edges of the triangles adds the finishing touch.

Skill Level: Intermediate

Size: Finished quilt is 90 × 96 inches

Fabrics and Supplies

- 6 yards of solid medium gray fabric
- 1 yard of fabric for binding (optional)
- ¼ yard *each* of 32 solid rainbow hues
- 8 yards of fabric for quilt back
- King-size quilt batting (120 inches square)
- Rotary cutter, ruler, and mat
- Template plastic (optional)

Cutting

These instructions are written for quick-cutting the more than 1,000 triangles required for this quilt. If you prefer to cut the pieces in a traditional manner, make a template using the measurements below (includes ¼-inch seam allowances):

- **A:** Make a 7¼-inch square; cut the square in half diagonally both ways.

From the solid medium gray fabric, cut:
- 512 A triangles

  Quick-Cutting Method: Cut twenty-six 7¼ × 44-inch strips. Cut each strip into 7¼-inch squares. You will need 128 squares. Cut each square in half diagonally in both directions to make four triangles. You will have eight extra triangles.

From each of the 32 solid rainbow hues, cut:
- 15 A triangles

  Quick-Cutting Method: Cut a 7¼ × 44-inch strip; from this strip cut four 7¼-inch squares. Cut each square in half diagonally in both directions to make four triangles. You will have one extra triangle in each color. Keep the triangles organized by making a stack for each color.

Assembling the Quilt Top

1. Determine how you will use your set of rainbow colors in the quilt. Use the photograph and the **Quilt Diagram** as reference. The 32 different colors run in vertical rows, with the position of the colors shifting from the left of the quilt to the right and from the top to the bottom. Compare the order of numbers from the first to the second vertical column in the **Quilt Diagram;** compare the second to the third column, and so on across the quilt. This shifting sequence of colors is what creates the rippling rainbow effect in the quilt. Make labels from 1 to 32 and pin a label onto each stack of triangles based on the desired color placement in the quilt. Use these numbers as reference as you lay out and assemble the quilt top.

2. Before laying out the pieces, fold each triangle in half and lightly crease it to form a centering guideline through the triangle. See **Diagram 1.** Use the line to position the triangles accurately from row to row.

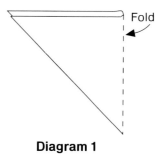

Diagram 1

3. Referring to the **Quilt Diagram,** lay out the colored and gray triangles in horizontal rows, with 15 colored triangles and 16 gray triangles per row. Match the numbers on your fabrics with the numbers that appear on the Quilt Diagram. The gray triangles at the right and left ends of the rows will be trimmed after the top is assembled.

4. Piece together the 15 colored triangles and 16 gray triangles for each row. Press the seam allowances toward the gray triangles.

5. Join the rows, matching the crease lines to the points of the triangles in the previous row. Press the seams in one direction. Refer to page 159 for instructions on assembling quilt tops.

6. Trim the gray triangles at the ends of the rows, using the crease lines as a guide. (NOTE: If you want to add binding strips to finish the quilt edges, you must allow for seam allowance as you trim. Mark a line ¼ inch outside each crease line to serve as a cutting guide. See Step 4 on page 106.)

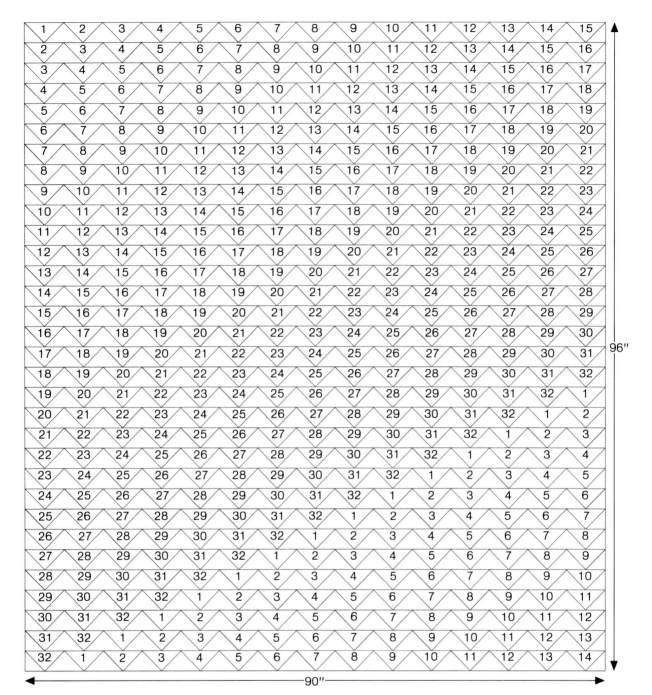

Quilt Diagram

Quilting and Finishing

1. To piece the quilt back, divide the 8 yards of backing fabric crosswise into three 96-inch lengths. Sew the pieces together along their long sides to create a backing that is about 96 by 126 inches.

2. Layer the backing, batting, and quilt top; baste.

3. Quilt as desired. The quilt shown is hand quilted ¼ inch along the inside of each colored triangle.

4. Finish the quilt by bringing the quilt top and backing together at the edges. First, trim the backing and batting even with the quilt top; then, trim away an extra ¼ inch of batting. Turn under the raw edges of the top and back about ¼ inch. Blindstitch the folded edges together by hand. If you prefer, you can finish the quilt in a more traditional manner by adding French-fold binding. See page 164 for instructions on making and attaching binding.

Lilies of the Field

This masterpiece is for the quilter who enjoys piecing, appliqué, and elaborate quilting. The blocks are a combination of patchwork and appliqué, and the quilted designs in the alternate blocks and outer border have extra padding, or *trapunto* work. Although this quilt requires a large investment of time, the end result will be a magnificent family heirloom.

Skill Level: Challenging

Size: Finished quilt is 78 × 109 inches
Finished block is 11 inches square

Fabrics and Supplies

- 9 yards of muslin for pieced blocks, setting blocks, and borders
- 3 yards of solid blue fabric for pieced blocks, pieced border, and binding
- 2½ yards of blue print fabric for pieced blocks and pieced border
- 7 yards of fabric for quilt back
- King-size quilt batting (120 inches square)
- Rotary cutter, ruler, and mat
- Template plastic
- Thread to match the appliqué fabrics
- White acrylic yarn and blunt needle for trapunto (optional)

Cutting

All measurements include ¼-inch seam allowances. Measurements for the borders are longer than needed; trim them to the exact length when they are added to the quilt top.

Make templates for pieces B, F, and G for the pieced blocks using the patterns on pages 113 and 114. Tips for making and using templates are on page 152. Turn the F template wrong-side up to cut F reverse pieces.

Directions for quick-cutting using a rotary cutter and a ruler are given for the remaining pattern pieces. Note that for some of the pieces, the quick-cutting method will result in leftover strips of fabric. If you prefer to cut all the pieces in a traditional manner, make additional templates for the following pieces (measurements include ¼-inch seam allowances):

- **A:** 1⅝-inch square
- **C and E:** Make a 2-inch square; cut the square in half diagonally.
- **D:** 2⅛-inch square
- **H:** 4¾-inch square
- **I:** Make a 3¼-inch square; cut the square in half diagonally in both directions.
- **J:** Make a 1⅞-inch square; cut the square in half diagonally.
- **K:** 1⅞-inch square

Before You Begin

To prepare the muslin, divide the yardage into one 3¼-yard (117-inch) length and one 5¾-yard (207-inch) length.

From the 117-inch length of muslin, cut:
- Two 6½ × 117-inch side border strips and two 6½ × 85-inch top and bottom border strips
- Ten 11½-inch setting blocks

From the 207-inch length of muslin, cut:
- Five 11½-inch setting blocks
- 16 side and end setting triangles

  Quick-Cutting Method: Cut four 16¾-inch squares. Cut each square in half diagonally in both directions to make four triangles.

- Four corner setting triangles

  Quick-Cutting Method: Cut two 8⅝-inch squares. Cut each square in half diagonally to make two triangles.

- 240 A squares

  Quick-Cutting Method: Cut ten 1⅝ × 44-inch strips; cut each strip into 1⅝-inch squares.

- 912 C triangles

  Quick-Cutting Method: Cut twenty-two 2 × 44-inch strips; cut each strip into 2-inch squares. You will need 456 squares. Cut each square in half diagonally to make two triangles.

- 48 E triangles

  Quick-Cutting Method: Cut three 2 × 44-inch strips; cut each strip into 2-inch squares. You will need 24 squares. Cut each square in half diagonally to make two triangles.

- 24 G pieces
- 24 H triangles

  Quick-Cutting Method: Cut two 4¾ × 44-inch strips; cut each strip into 4¾-inch squares. You will need 12 squares. Cut each square in half diagonally to make two triangles.

- 656 J triangles

  Quick-Cutting Method: Cut sixteen 1⅞ × 44-inch strips; cut each strip into 1⅞-inch squares. You will need 328 squares. Cut each square in half diagonally to make two triangles.

From the solid blue fabric, cut:
- 576 B diamonds

- 48 E triangles

  Quick-Cutting Method: Cut two 2 × 44-inch strips; cut the strip into 2-inch squares. You will need 24 squares. Cut each square in half diagonally to make two triangles.

- 24 F pieces and 24 F reverse pieces
- Twenty-four ¾ × 15-inch bias strips
- 152 I triangles

  Quick-Cutting Method: Cut three 3¼ × 44-inch strips; cut each strip into 3¼-inch squares. You will need 38 squares. Cut each square in half diagonally in both directions to make four triangles.

- 8 K squares for pieced border

  Quick-Cutting Method: Cut a 1⅞ × 44-inch strip; cut the strip into 1⅞-inch squares.

From the blue print fabric, cut:

- 576 B diamonds
- 72 D squares

  Quick-Cutting Method: Cut four 2⅛ × 44-inch strips; cut each strip into 2⅛-inch squares.

- 160 I triangles

  Quick-Cutting Method: Cut four 3¼ × 44-inch strips; cut each strip into 3¼-inch squares. You will need 40 squares. Cut each square in half diagonally in both directions to make four triangles.

Making the Blocks

Each block is made up of four different sections; you will need a total of 24 pieced blocks to make this quilt. Refer to the **Fabric Key**, the **Block Diagram,** and **Diagrams 1** through **10** to piece the blocks. When possible, press the seams toward the darker fabric.

Fabric Key

 Solid blue

 Blue print

 Muslin

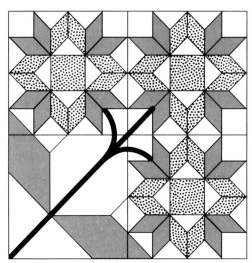

Block Diagram

To prepare the bias strips for stems, press the 15-inch bias pieces in thirds, as shown in the general bias instructions on page 157. Cut each pressed strip into one 10-inch and two 2½-inch pieces.

Section 1

1. Sew four muslin C triangles to a blue print D square, as shown in **Diagram 1.**

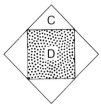

Diagram 1

2. Sew eight solid blue B diamonds together in pairs, making a total of four pairs. Referring to **Diagram 2,** add a blue print B diamond to each side of the solid two-diamond units.

Diagram 2

3. Set in a muslin C triangle along each side of the four-diamond units, as shown in **Diagram 3.** Refer to page 155 for instructions on setting-in pieces.

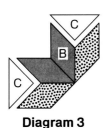

Diagram 3

4. Set a muslin A square into the corner of three of the diamond units. Leave the seams of one corner square open, as shown in **Diagram 4.** You will insert the stem into this seam after the sections are sewn together.

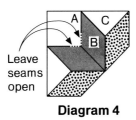

Leave seams open

Diagram 4

5. Combine a muslin E triangle and a solid blue E triangle to make a corner square for the fourth four-diamond unit. Set in the corner square, as shown in **Diagram 5.**

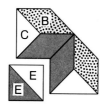

Diagram 5

6. Referring to **Diagram 6,** sew the diamond units to the center CD unit. Make 24 of these sections.

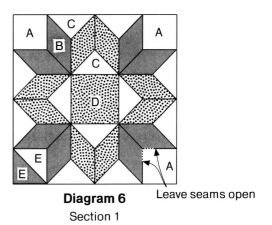

Diagram 6
Leave seams open
Section 1

Section 2

1. Follow the same procedure as for Section 1, but use a muslin A square at each corner of the section. Leave the corner seams of one A square open for the bias stem, as shown in **Diagram 7.** Make 24 of these sections.

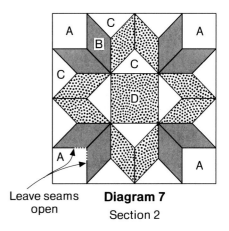

Leave seams open
Diagram 7
Section 2

Section 3

1. Follow the same procedure as for Section 1. In this section, use the muslin and solid blue pieced corner square as indicated in **Diagram 8.** Leave the seams of one muslin A square open, as shown in the diagram. Make 24 of these sections.

Leave seams open

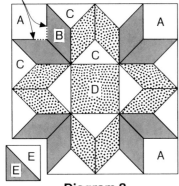

Diagram 8

Section 3

Section 4

1. Sew an F and F reverse to opposite sides of a G piece. Set a muslin C triangle into the sides of the unit, as shown in **Diagram 9.** Add an H triangle at the corner. Repeat to make 24 sections.

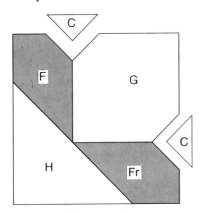

Diagram 9

Section 4

Joining the Sections

1. Lay out the four sections, as shown in **Diagram 10,** and stitch them together. Repeat to make a total of 24 blocks.

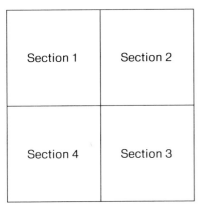

Section 1	Section 2
Section 4	Section 3

Diagram 10

2. Referring to the **Block Diagram** for correct placement, baste the pressed bias stems in position, inserting the ends in the seams you left open. Hand stitch the seams closed using a blind hem stitch. Place the other ends of the short stems under the long stem.

3. Appliqué the stems in place using matching thread. See page 156 for tips on appliqué.

Assembling the Quilt Top

1. Referring to the **Quilt Diagram** and the photograph, combine pieced blocks, setting blocks, side setting triangles, and corner triangles in diagonal rows to form the inner quilt top. When joining blocks, press seams in opposite directions from row to row so you can easily align the seams when you join the rows. Refer to page 159 for instructions on assembling quilt tops. The inner quilt should measure $62\frac{1}{2} \times 93\frac{1}{2}$ inches, including seam allowances.

2. To piece the Goose Chase border units, stitch muslin J triangles to two sides of an I triangle, as shown in **Diagram 11.** Make 152 units with solid I triangles and 160 units with print I triangles. Press the seams away from the I triangles.

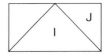

Diagram 11

Goose Chase Border Unit

3. Stitch a muslin J triangle to each side of a solid blue K square, as shown in **Diagram 12.** Make eight of these square border units. These will be used at the corners and at the center of the side and end borders.

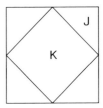

Diagram 12

Square Border Unit

Quilt Diagram

4. To make the two side borders, construct four strips of alternating print and solid border units, using 24 print units and 23 solid units in each strip. The strips will have print units at both ends. Make sure all the I triangles are pointing in the same direction.

5. Sew one of the four pieced border strips to the side of a square border unit, making sure the I triangles point away from the square. Sew another of the strips to the opposite side of the square unit, again making sure the I triangles point away from the square, as shown in **Diagram 13.** Make a second border the same way.

Diagram 13

Side Border Strip

6. Compare the border strips to the long sides of the quilt top. If necessary, adjust the length by either taking in or letting out seams or by adding or deleting units. Sew the completed border strips to the sides of the quilt. Press the border seams toward the inner quilt.

7. In the same manner, construct four border strips for the top and bottom of the quilt, using 16 print border units and 15 solid blue units per strip. The strips will have print units at both ends.

8. Sew one of the four pieced border strips to the side of a square border unit, pointing the triangles away from the square. Sew a second strip to the opposite side of the square, again making sure the triangles point away from the square. Make a second border strip the same way.

9. Compare the border strips to the top and bottom of the quilt top and adjust the length as needed. Sew a square border unit to each end of the border strip.

10. Attach the borders to the top and bottom of the quilt top.

11. Measure your quilt top, trim the outer muslin border strips as needed, attach, and miter the corners. Refer to page 159 for tips on adding and mitering borders. Press the seams toward the muslin borders.

Quilting and Finishing

1. Mark quilting designs as desired on the finished quilt top. The quilt shown has outline quilting in the ditch in the pieced blocks, a design of grape clusters and leaves in the alternate blocks, and feathers in the muslin borders. A small diagonal grid of squares, called crosshatching, is quilted in all open spaces. Trapunto was added to the alternate block design and the border feathers. The **Grape Cluster Quilting Design** for the alternate blocks is on page 114. See **Diagram 14** for placement within the block. See "Adding Trapunto for Extra Elegance" on page 24 for tips on trapunto.

Diagram 14

2. Layer the backing, batting, and quilt top; baste.

3. Quilt all marked designs.

4. Make French-fold binding from the remaining solid blue fabric. You will need approximately 380 inches (10½ yards) of binding. Refer to page 164 for instructions on making and attaching binding.

5. Sew the binding to the quilt top. Trim excess batting and backing. Turn the binding to the back of the quilt and hand stitch in place.

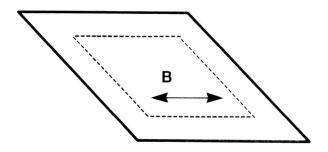

F

G

Center Flower Quilting Design

Grape Cluster Quilting Design

Here Comes the Sun

Peering out from the center of this medallion quilt is the sun, surrounded by four dramatic pieced borders. Sun-warmed tones of orange and red combine with cool purples and blues to suggest the colors of a sunrise. Quilted sunshine faces carry out the sunrise theme in a playful way.

Skill Level: Intermediate

Size: Finished quilt is 42 inches square

Fabrics and Supplies

- 1½ yards of solid black fabric for the outer border and quilt back
- ¾ yard of solid light blue fabric for the fourth border
- ½ yard *each* of the following five solid-color fabrics: dark red for the fourth border; red-orange and medium light purple for the third border; and medium orange and medium purple for the second border
- ¼ yard *each* of the following three solid-color fabrics: light orange and dark purple for the first border; and dark orange for the center square
- Quilt batting, larger than 42 inches square
- Rotary cutter, ruler, and mat
- Template plastic

Cutting

All measurements and pattern pieces include ¼-inch seam allowances. Cut the largest fabric pieces first; then cut the smaller pieces from the remaining fabric.

Prepare plastic templates for triangle B and pattern piece C using the full-size patterns on pages 118 and 119. Instructions for making and using templates are on page 152.

From the solid black fabric, cut:
- Four 1½ × 44-inch strips for the outer border
- Reserve the remaining fabric for the quilt back

From the solid light blue fabric, cut:
- 28 B triangles
- 4 C pieces

From the solid dark red fabric, cut:
- 32 B triangles

From the solid red-orange fabric, cut:
- 24 B triangles

From the solid medium light purple fabric, cut:
- 20 B triangles
- 4 C pieces

From the solid medium orange fabric, cut:
- 16 B triangles

From the solid medium purple fabric, cut:
- 12 B triangles
- 4 C pieces

From the solid light orange fabric, cut:
- 8 B triangles

From the solid dark purple fabric, cut:
- 4 B triangles
- 4 C pieces

From the solid dark orange fabric, cut:
- One 8½-inch A square for the quilt center

Piecing and Adding the First Border

1. Referring to **Diagram 1** and the **Fabric Key,** make a pieced border section by stitching a light orange B triangle to each long side of a dark purple B triangle. Make four of these border sections.

Fabric Key

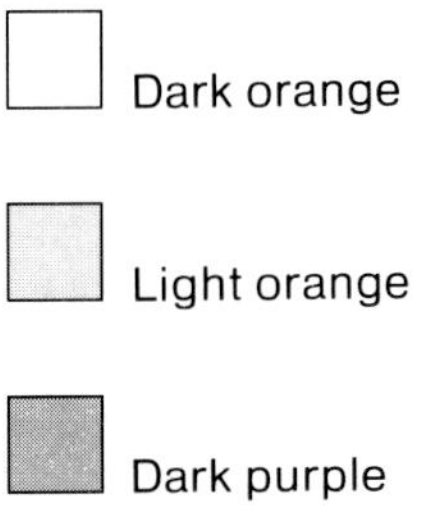

Dark orange

Light orange

Dark purple

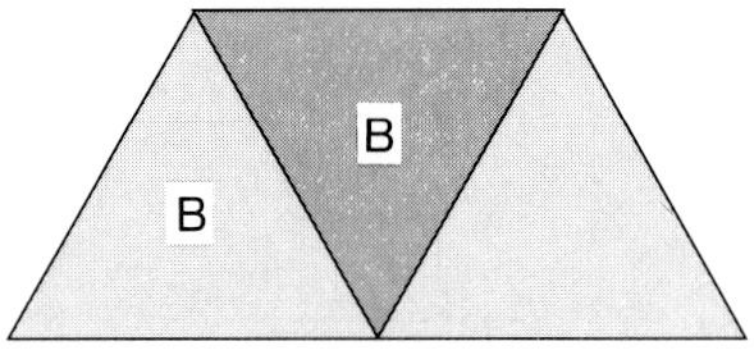

Diagram 1

2. Referring to **Diagram 2,** sew a border section to each side of the center A square. Start and stop your stitching ¼ inch from the ends of the pieces, leaving the seam allowances free at the corners. This will make it easier to set in the C pieces. Sew all four border pieces to the sides of the square. Press the seam allowances away from the quilt center.

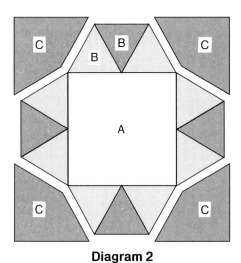

Diagram 2

3. Set a dark purple C piece into each corner of the border, as shown in **Diagram 2.** See page 155 for tips on setting-in pieces.

Piecing and Adding the Other Borders

1. Referring to the **Quilt Diagram,** stitch together and add the remaining pieced borders in the same way you added the first border. For the second border, stitch border sections by sewing together four medium orange B triangles and three medium purple B triangles. Add the borders to the quilt and set in the corresponding C pieces.

2. For the third border, stitch border sections by sewing together six red-orange B triangles and five medium light purple B triangles. Add the borders to the quilt and set in the corresponding C pieces.

3. For the fourth border, stitch border sections by sewing together eight dark red B triangles and seven light blue B triangles. Add the borders to the quilt and set in the corresponding C pieces.

Adding the Outer Border

1. Sew a black border strip to each side of the quilt top, as shown in the **Quilt Diagram.** Miter the

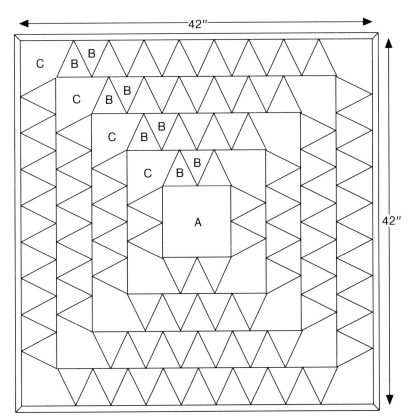

Quilt Diagram

border corner seams. Press the seam allowances toward the black borders. Refer to page 159 for instructions on adding and mitering borders.

Quilting and Finishing

1. Mark quilting designs onto the quilt top with a pencil or other removable marker. The quilt shown has a large sun design in the center square and a slightly different small sun design in each C piece. The pattern for the **Center Sun Quilting Design** is on page 120. Patterns for four different **Small Sun Quilting Designs** are provided on page 121. You can use the designs provided or modify them to create your own designs.

2. On the purple and light blue B triangles, mark lines spaced ½ inch apart, parallel to one side of the triangles, as shown in the photograph. In the orange and dark red B triangles, mark gently curved lines spaced ½ inch apart, as shown.

3. Layer the quilt back, batting, and quilt top; baste.

4. Hand or machine quilt on all the marked quilting lines. The quilt shown was hand quilted with various colors of quilting thread chosen to match the fabric pieces.

5. When the quilting is complete, trim the quilt back and batting even with the quilt top. Trim away an extra ¼ inch of batting so the batting is ¼ inch from the fabric edges. Turn in ¼ inch on the quilt top and quilt back. Blindstitch the folded edges together around the perimeter of the quilt. See page 167 for instructions on making and attaching a hanging sleeve.

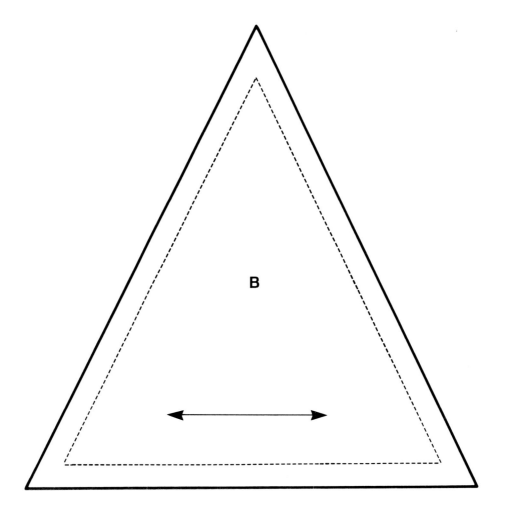

B

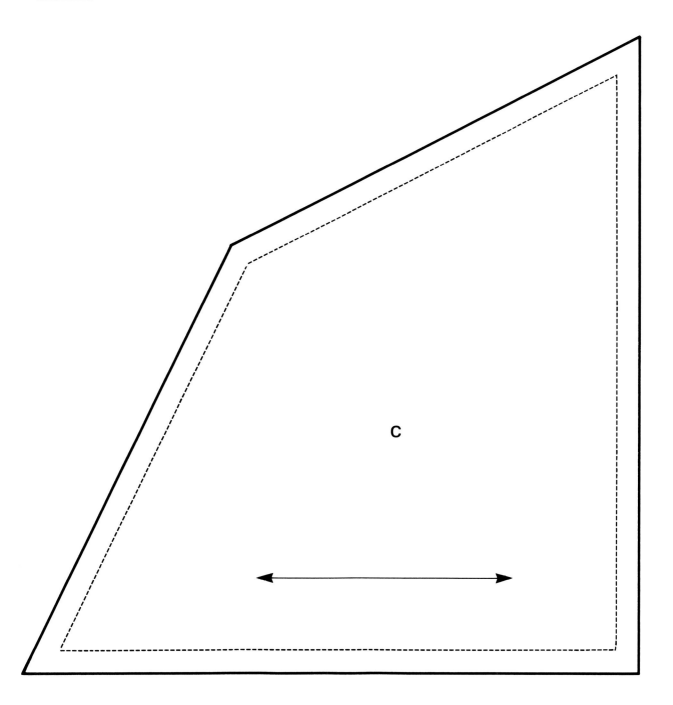

c

Center Sun Quilting Design

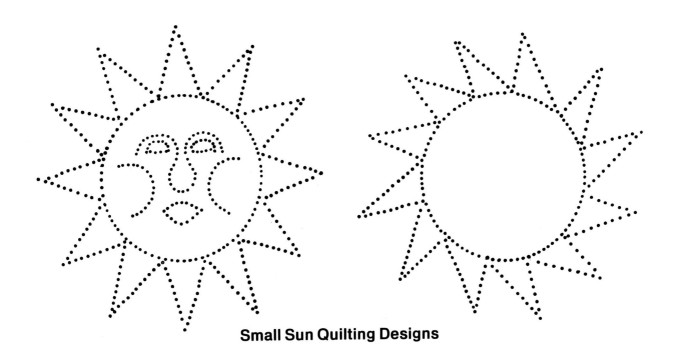

Small Sun Quilting Designs

HOLIDAYS
and
CELEBRATIONS

Hearts and Vines Table Runner

Lace and ribbons accent the pretty appliqué hearts and curving vines of this easy and elegant table runner. Make one for yourself and one for a special friend as a quick Valentine's Day gift. Play with different color variations to see what happens. Light hearts on a darker background would create a whole new dramatic look.

Skill Level: Easy

Size: Finished table runner is approximately 15 × 49 inches, excluding the lace edging

Fabrics and Supplies

- 1½ yards of white-on-cream print muslin
- ⅝ yard of green print fabric
- ¼ yard of red print fabric
- 3¾ yards of 1½-inch-wide insertion lace
- 4½ yards of green satin ribbon to fit insertion lace
- Polyester fleece or other low-loft batting, 18 × 52 inches
- Rotary cutter, ruler, and mat
- Template plastic
- Tracing paper
- Black permanent felt-tip pen
- Blunt needle with eye large enough to thread with ribbon
- Thread to match the appliqué fabrics

Cutting

Make plastic templates for the heart and leaf appliqué patterns from the **Single Heart Design** on page 127. The patterns are finished size and do not include seam allowances; add seam allowances when cutting pieces from the fabric. Instructions for making and using templates are on page 152.

From the white-on-cream print muslin, cut:
- One 15½ × 49½-inch rectangle for the front of the runner
- One 18 × 52-inch rectangle for the back of the runner

From the green print fabric, cut:
- Three 1¾ × 25-inch bias strips for the vines
- 28 leaves

From the red print fabric, cut:
- 16 hearts

Appliquéing the Design

1. On tracing paper, make full-size patterns of the appliqué designs to use as placement guides for the appliqué pieces. For the center design, fold a piece of tracing paper at least 12 inches square into fourths, and trace the **Center Heart Design** on page 126 in each quadrant. Using a permanent pen, darken the design outlines. Follow the same procedure to make a full-size pattern for the **Four-Heart Design** on page 127. Trace the **Single Heart Design** onto a piece of tracing paper and darken the lines.

2. To create positioning lines for the appliqué designs, fold the piece of muslin for the front of the runner in half lengthwise and crosswise, and lightly press.

3. Position the tracing paper drawing of the center design under the center of the muslin runner front. Using a pencil, chalk, or other removable marker, lightly trace the **Center Heart Design** onto the right side of the runner front. In a similar manner, trace the **Four-Heart Design** at each end of the runner front so that the center of the design is positioned approximately 5½ inches in from the end.

4. Prepare the hearts and leaves for appliqué, using the heart and leaf shapes from the **Single Heart Design** as appliqué patterns. Be sure to add seam allowances when cutting out the appliqué pieces. See page 156 for general instructions on hand appliqué.

5. Prepare the bias pieces for appliqué by pressing the strips in thirds, as shown on page 158. The pressed strips should be approximately ½ inch to ⅝ inch wide. From one of the prepared bias strips, cut four 5-inch-long pieces for the center design.

6. Baste the short bias vine sections along the guidelines in the **Center Heart Design.** Pin or baste the 4 hearts and 12 leaves in place.

7. For the **Four-Heart Designs** at the ends of the runner, baste hearts and leaves within the positioning guidelines.

8. Referring to the photograph, curve a long vine piece between the **Center Heart Design** and each **Four-Heart Design.** Baste the vines in place. Tuck the ends of the vine under other appliqué pieces and trim off any excess vine.

9. Again referring to the photograph, trace positioning guidelines for two **Single Heart Designs** along each long, curved section of the vine. Baste the hearts and leaves within the guidelines.

10. Using thread to match the appliqué pieces, appliqué the hearts, vines, and leaves.

Quilting and Finishing

1. Fold the runner front in fourths by folding in half lengthwise and crosswise. Trim the ends of the runner so they form a gentle curve; open the folds.

2. Mark a background grid of 1-inch diamonds on the muslin on the runner front.

3. Layer the runner back, batting, and runner front; securely baste the layers together. Baste through all layers, approximately ½ inch from the edge, around the perimeter of the runner front.

4. Trim the batting and runner back even with the runner front. Trim away an extra ¼ inch of batting. Turn in ¼ inch of the runner front and runner back.

5. Pin the folded edges together, catching insertion lace between the layers. You may need to gently gather the lace in some areas to allow enough fullness so it won't curl at the outer edge. Hand stitch the edge closed.

6. Outline quilt around all of the appliqué pieces; quilt the grid of diamonds.

7. Cut the ribbon into four equal pieces. Thread a needle with a length of ribbon. Beginning at the center of one side of the runner, insert the ribbon in the lace, bringing it out at the middle of the runner end. Repeat to insert the other pieces of ribbon. Tie the free ends of the ribbon in small bows where they meet; trim the excess ribbon. Secure the ties with a few stitches so the bows do not come undone when the runner is washed.

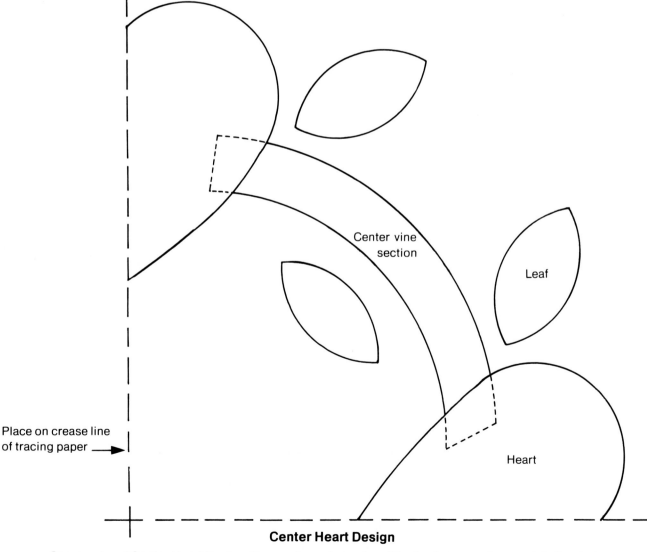

Place on crease line of tracing paper ⟶

Center vine section

Leaf

Heart

Center Heart Design

One-quarter of **Center Heart Design.** Trace onto each quarter of the tracing paper to complete the design.

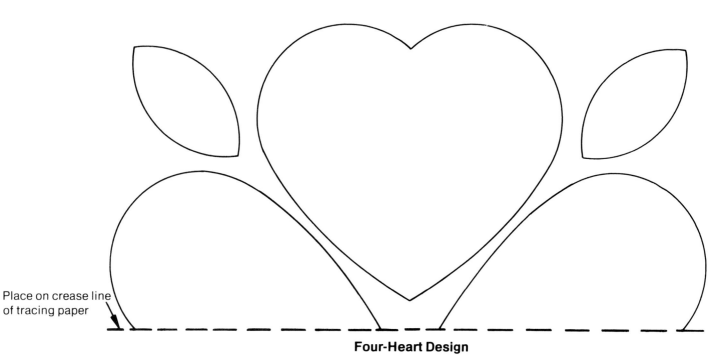

Place on crease line
of tracing paper

Four-Heart Design

One-half of **Four Heart Design.** Trace onto each half of the tracing paper to complete the design.

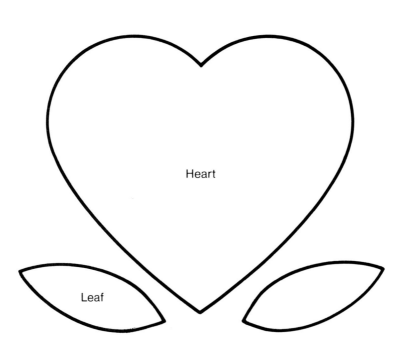

Heart

Leaf

Single Heart Design

Something's Fishy

Stitch up this wonderfully whimsical quilt for a special little person in your life. What a great way to celebrate a birthday or to commemorate a milestone like learning how to swim! Its bright colors and fun shapes are sure to bring a smile. Hidden under the waves are two surprises: There's one fish looking straight at you, and one heading in the wrong direction! Can you spot them?

Skill Level: Easy

Size: Finished quilt is $36\frac{5}{8} \times 42\frac{1}{4}$ inches
Each finished square is 2 inches

Fabrics and Supplies

- 1 yard *each* of red pindot and solid royal blue fabrics
- $\frac{5}{8}$ yard of light blue print fabric
- $\frac{1}{2}$ yard of solid light blue fabric
- $\frac{1}{4}$ yard *each* of solid white, yellow pindot, purple pindot, and orange pindot fabrics
- $\frac{1}{8}$ yard *each* of bright green dot, pale green dot, and red print fabrics
- $1\frac{3}{8}$ yards of fabric for quilt back
- Crib-size quilt batting (45×60 inches)
- Rotary cutter, ruler, and mat
- Brown embroidery floss
- Template plastic (optional)

Cutting

All measurements include $\frac{1}{4}$-inch seam allowances. The instructions below are written for quick-cutting the various quilt pieces using a rotary cutter and a ruler. Note that for some of the pieces, the quick-cutting method will result in leftover strips of fabric. If you prefer to cut the pieces traditionally, make templates for the following pieces:

- **A:** $2\frac{1}{2}$-inch square
- **B:** Make a $2\frac{7}{8}$-inch square; cut the square in half diagonally.
- **C:** Make a $3\frac{1}{4}$-inch square; cut the square in half diagonally in both directions.
- **D:** Make a $3\frac{3}{4}$-inch square; cut the square in half diagonally.

From the red pindot fabric, cut:
- Four $1\frac{7}{8} \times 44$-inch border strips
- 10 A squares

  Quick-Cutting Method: Cut a $2\frac{1}{2} \times 44$-inch strip. From this strip, cut ten $2\frac{1}{2}$-inch squares.
- 10 B triangles

  Quick-Cutting Method: Cut a $2\frac{7}{8} \times 44$-inch strip. From this strip, cut five $2\frac{7}{8}$-inch squares. Cut each square in half diagonally to make two triangles.

- 1 C triangle

  Quick-Cutting Method: Cut a $3\frac{1}{4}$-inch square. Cut the square in half diagonally in both directions to make four triangles. You will have three extra triangles.
- Reserve the remaining fabric for binding

From the solid royal blue fabric, cut:
- 37 A squares

  Quick-Cutting Method: Cut three $2\frac{1}{2} \times 44$-inch strips. From the strips, cut thirty-seven $2\frac{1}{2}$-inch squares.
- 127 B triangles

  Quick-Cutting Method: Cut five $2\frac{7}{8} \times 44$-inch strips. From these strips, cut sixty-four $2\frac{7}{8}$-inch squares. Cut each square in half diagonally to make two triangles. You will have one extra triangle.
- 26 D triangles

  Quick-Cutting Method: Cut two $3\frac{3}{4} \times 44$-inch strips. From the strips, cut thirteen $3\frac{3}{4}$-inch squares. Cut each square in half diagonally to make two triangles.

From the light blue print fabric, cut:
- 65 A squares

  Quick-Cutting Method: Cut four $2\frac{1}{2} \times 44$-inch strips. From the strips, cut sixty-five $2\frac{1}{2}$-inch squares.
- 16 B triangles

  Quick-Cutting Method: Cut a $2\frac{7}{8} \times 44$-inch strip. From this strip, cut eight $2\frac{7}{8}$-inch squares. Cut each square in half diagonally to make two triangles.
- 11 C triangles

  Quick-Cutting Method: Cut a $3\frac{1}{4} \times 44$-inch strip. From the strip, cut three $3\frac{1}{4}$-inch squares. Cut each square in half diagonally in both directions to make four triangles. You will have one extra triangle.
- 2 D triangles

  Quick-Cutting Method: Cut a $3\frac{3}{4}$-inch square. Cut the square in half diagonally to make two triangles.

From the solid light blue fabric, cut:
- 44 A squares

  Quick-Cutting Method: Cut three $2\frac{1}{2} \times 44$-inch strips. From the strips, cut forty-four $2\frac{1}{2}$-inch squares.

- 7 B triangles

  Quick-Cutting Method: Cut a 2⅞ × 44-inch strip. From this strip, cut four 2⅞-inch squares. Cut each square in half diagonally to make two triangles. You will have one extra triangle.

From the solid white fabric, cut:

- 4 A squares

  Quick-Cutting Method: Cut a 2½ × 44-inch strip. From the strip, cut four 2½-inch squares.

- 11 B triangles

  Quick-Cutting Method: Cut a 2⅞ × 44-inch strip. From this strip, cut six 2⅞-inch squares. Cut each square in half diagonally to make two triangles. You will have one extra triangle.

- 10 C triangles

  Quick-Cutting Method: Cut a 3¼ × 44-inch strip. From the strip, cut three 3¼-inch squares. Cut each square in half diagonally both ways to make four triangles. You will have two extra triangles.

From the yellow pindot fabric, cut:

- 11 A squares

  Quick-Cutting Method: Cut a 2½ × 44-inch strip. From the strip, cut eleven 2½-inch squares.

- 11 B triangles

  Quick-Cutting Method: Cut a 2⅞ × 44-inch strip. From this strip, cut six 2⅞-inch squares. Cut each square in half diagonally to make two triangles. You will have one extra triangle.

From the purple pindot fabric, cut:

- 11 A squares

  Quick-Cutting Method: Cut a 2½ × 44-inch strip. From the strip, cut eleven 2½-inch squares.

- 11 B triangles

  Quick-Cutting Method: Cut a 2⅞ × 44-inch strip. From this strip, cut six 2⅞-inch squares. Cut each square in half diagonally to make two triangles. You will have one extra triangle.

From the orange pindot fabric, cut:

- 10 A squares

Quick-Cutting Method: Cut a 2½ × 44-inch strip. From the strip, cut ten 2½-inch squares.

- 10 B triangles

  Quick-Cutting Method: Cut a 2⅞ × 44-inch strip. From this strip, cut five 2⅞-inch squares. Cut each square in half diagonally to make two triangles.

From the bright green dot fabric, cut:

- 16 B triangles

  Quick-Cutting Method: Cut a 2⅞ × 44-inch strip. From this strip, cut eight 2⅞-inch squares. Cut each square in half diagonally to make two triangles.

From the pale green dot fabric, cut:

- 8 B triangles

  Quick-Cutting Method: Cut a 2⅞ × 44-inch strip. From this strip, cut four 2⅞-inch squares. Cut each square in half diagonally to make two triangles.

From the red print fabric, cut:

- 2 A squares

  Quick-Cutting Method: Cut two 2½-inch squares.

- 7 B triangles

  Quick-Cutting Method: Cut a 2⅞ × 44-inch strip. From this strip, cut four 2⅞-inch squares. Cut each square in half diagonally to make two triangles. You will have one extra triangle.

Piecing the Triangle Units

1. Join pairs of B triangles to make the two-triangle units shown in **Diagram 1.** Refer to the table below to determine which color triangles should be sewn together and how many of each combination you will need.

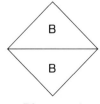

Diagram 1
Two-Triangle Unit

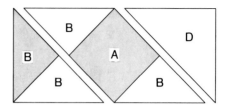

TWO-TRIANGLE UNITS

Fabrics	Number of Units Needed
Light blue print/white	1
Solid light blue/purple pindot	1
Solid light blue/orange pindot	1
Royal blue/bright green dot	13
Royal blue/pale green dot	6
Royal blue/red pindot	5
Royal blue/yellow pindot	4
Royal blue/purple pindot	3
Royal blue/orange pindot	2
Bright green dot/pale green dot	1

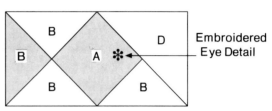

Border Unit Piecing Diagram

2. To make the three-triangle units shown in **Diagram 2,** first join a light blue print C triangle and a white C triangle into a larger triangle. Then, sew a white B triangle to the long side of this pieced triangle, as shown. Make nine of these three-triangle units. Make one three-triangle unit using a light blue print C triangle, a red pindot C triangle, and a light blue print B triangle.

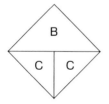

Diagram 2
Three-Triangle Unit

Piecing the Fish Borders

1. Refer to the **Border Unit Piecing Diagram** to piece the 26 fish border units using pattern pieces A, B, and D. The background color on all the border units is royal blue. You will need seven border units *each* in yellow pindot, purple pindot, and orange pindot. You will need five border units in red pindot.

2. Referring to the **Fabric Key** and the **Quilt Diagram,** sew fish units together into the four pieced borders. Pin labels from 1 to 4 on borders, as indicated in the diagram, and set the borders aside.

Assembling the Quilt Top

1. Referring to the **Quilt Diagram,** lay out the A squares, B triangles, C triangles, D triangles, two-triangle units and three-triangle units. Note that in the quilt shown, the wrong side of the light blue print was used in some places to create the effect of a cloud. If you want to duplicate this effect, simply turn the squares wrong-side up, as shown in the **Quilt Diagram.**

2. Sew the pieces together in diagonal rows, pressing the seam allowances in opposite directions from row to row. Join the rows. Refer to page 159 for instructions on assembling quilt tops.

3. Sew red pindot border strips to the sides of the quilt; trim even with the top and bottom edges. Sew red pindot border strips to the top and bottom of the quilt; trim.

4. Referring to **Diagram 3,** pin Border 1 to the top edge of the quilt, with the left edge of the border even with the upper left edge of the quilt. Sew the border on, stitching in the direction of the arrow, as

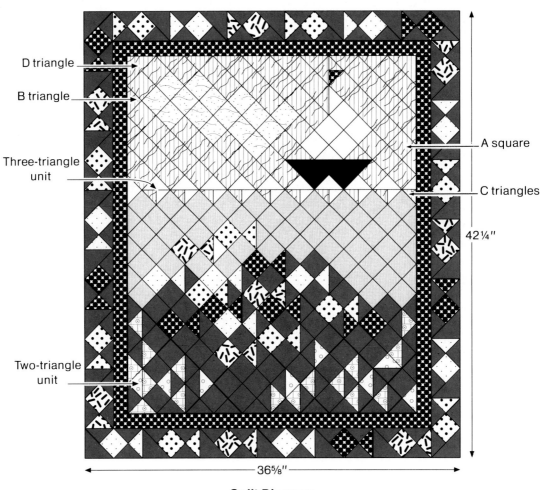

D triangle

B triangle

Three-triangle unit

Two-triangle unit

A square

C triangles

42¼"

36⅝"

Quilt Diagram

Fabric Key

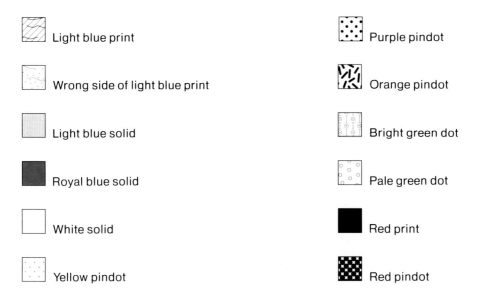

Light blue print

Wrong side of light blue print

Light blue solid

Royal blue solid

White solid

Yellow pindot

Purple pindot

Orange pindot

Bright green dot

Pale green dot

Red print

Red pindot

shown in **Diagram 3,** but stop the stitching about 5 inches from the end. This will allow you to avoid having to set in border pieces. The final stitching will be completed after Border 4 has been added.

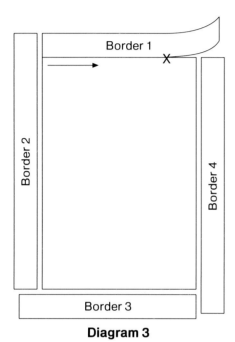

Diagram 3

5. Sew Border 2 to the left side of the quilt and the edge of Border 1. Sew Border 3 to the bottom of the quilt and the edge of Border 2. Finally, sew Border 4 to the right side of the quilt and the edge of Border 3.

6. Stitch the unsewn end of Border 1 to the top edge of the quilt and across the top of Border 4.

Quilting and Finishing

1. Layer the quilt back, batting, and quilt top; baste.

2. Quilt as desired. The quilt shown was machine quilted in a random pattern with clear nylon monofilament thread. For tips on this technique, see page 163. Referring to the photograph and the **Border Unit Piecing Diagram,** hand stitch an eye (or two!) on each fish using the brown embroidery floss. Stitch a simple star shape using a horizontal, a vertical, and two diagonal overlapping stitches. Be careful not to stitch through to the back side of the quilt.

3. Make French-fold binding from the remaining red pindot fabric. You will need approximately 166 inches (4⅝ yards) of binding. Sew the binding to the quilt, mitering the corners. See page 159 for instructions on adding and mitering borders. Instructions for making and attaching binding are on page 164. Instructions for making and attaching a hanging sleeve can be found on page 167.

Holiday Place Mat Set

Make these festive holiday place mats and matching mug mats to welcome in the Christmas season or to give as a special gift to someone on your list. Using machine appliqué and strip piecing, you can stitch them together in no time.

Skill Level: Easy

Size: Finished place mats are 13 ×
18 inches
Finished mug mats are 5 inches square
Materials will make two place mats and two
mug mats

Fabrics and Supplies

- 1 yard of solid cranberry fabric
- ⅝ yard of red-and-green plaid fabric
- ¼ yard of solid green fabric
- ⅛ yard of solid white fabric
- ⅛ yard *each* of two green print fabrics
- ⅛ yard *each* of two red print fabrics
- ¾ yard of polyester fleece
- ¼ yard of paper-backed fusible webbing for machine appliqué
- Rotary cutter, ruler, and mat
- Template plastic
- Gold metallic thread
- Thread to match the appliqué fabrics

Cutting

The measurements for the place mat and mug mat pieces include ¼-inch seam allowances. Since the pieces needed to make these projects are strips, squares, and rectangles, no patterns are given. Cut the fabric pieces with a rotary cutter and a ruler, or measure and mark the pieces with a ruler and cut them with scissors. Note that for some of the pieces, the quick-cutting method will result in leftover strips of fabric.

The patterns for the bell and tree templates on page 138 do not include seam allowances. If you plan to appliqué by hand rather than machine, be sure to add seam allowances when cutting the appliqué pieces from your fabric. Tips for making and using templates appear on page 152.

From the solid cranberry fabric, cut:
- Two 14 × 19-inch rectangles for the place mat backs
- One 11½ × 13½-inch rectangle for the tree place mat
- Two 2½ × 13½-inch strips

Quick-Cutting Method: Cut a 2½ × 44-inch strip. From this strip, cut two 13½-inch segments.
- Reserve the remaining fabric for bells

From the red-and-green plaid fabric, cut:
- Four 2¼ × 44-inch strips for binding
- Three 1 × 44-inch strips
- Two 5½-inch squares for the mug mat backs

Quick-Cutting Method: Cut a 5½ × 44-inch strip. From this strip, cut two 5½-inch squares.

From the solid green fabric, cut:
- One 2½ × 13½-inch strip for the bell place mat
- Reserve the remaining fabric for trees

From the solid white fabric, cut:
- Eight 3½-inch squares for appliqué background

Quick-Cutting Method: Cut a 3½ × 44-inch strip. From this strip, cut eight 3½-inch squares.

From the first green print fabric, cut:
- One 2½ × 13½-inch strip for the bell place mat
- Eight 1 × 3½-inch rectangles

Quick-Cutting Method: Cut a 1 × 44-inch strip. From this strip, cut eight 3½-inch-long segments.

From the second green print fabric, cut:
- One 2½ × 13½-inch strip for the bell place mat
- Eight 1 × 4-inch rectangles

Quick-Cutting Method: Cut a 1 × 44-inch strip. From this strip, cut eight 4-inch-long segments.

From the first red print fabric, cut:
- One 2½ × 13½-inch strip for the bell place mat
- Eight 1 × 4-inch rectangles

Quick-Cutting Method: Cut a 1 × 44-inch strip. From this strip, cut eight 4-inch-long segments.

From the second red print fabric, cut:
- One 2½ × 13½-inch strip for the bell place mat

■ Eight 1 × 4½-inch rectangles

Quick-Cutting Method: Cut a 1 × 44-inch strip. From this strip, cut eight 4½-inch-long segments.

From the polyester fleece, cut:
■ Two 14 × 19-inch rectangles
■ Two 5½-inch squares

Making the Appliquéd Sections

1. Refer to page 158 for instructions on appliquéing with fusible webbing. Cut four trees and four bells from the reserved fabric using the **Tree Appliqué Pattern** and the **Bell Appliqué Pattern** on page 138. Following the manufacturer's instructions, fuse each tree and bell to the center of a white background square. If you prefer to hand appliqué the pieces, you don't need to fuse them, but be sure to add seam allowances before cutting the shapes from the fabric. Tips on hand appliqué appear on page 156.

2. Using matching thread, hand or machine appliqué the shapes to the background squares. Instructions for machine appliqué are on page 158.

3. Embellish the appliqués by hand with metallic thread, as shown in **Diagrams 1** and **2**. Satin stitch a clapper on each bell and embroider decorations on the bells and trees. To make the bell clapper, you will be adding hand stitches on top of the machine appliqué stitches.

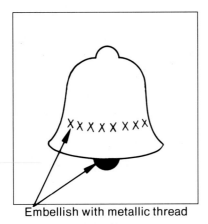

Embellish with metallic thread

Diagram 1

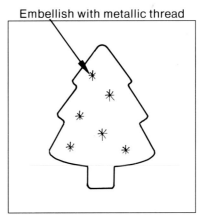

Embellish with metallic thread

Diagram 2

4. Trim the squares with Log Cabin patchwork, as shown in **Diagram 3**. The most efficient way to do this is to use the assembly-line method: Lay out all the appliqué squares and the Log Cabin strips and do the same step on all the squares at the same time. After each strip is added, press the seam allowance away from the center. Begin by sewing a 3½-inch-long green print strip to the right side of all squares. Add a 4-inch-long red print strip to the top of the squares. Sew a 4-inch-long green print strip to the left side of all the squares. Finally, sew a 4½-inch-long red print strip to the bottom of all the squares.

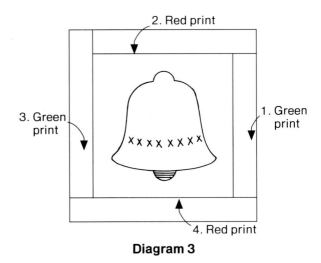

Diagram 3

5. For the place mats, sew together three matching trimmed squares in a vertical row to create a long rectangle. Make one rectangle with three bells and one with three trees. The completed rectangles should measure 4½ × 12½ inches, including seam allowances. Save the remaining trimmed squares for the mug mats.

6. Sew a 1 × 44-inch plaid strip to the short side of one rectangle, then trim the strip even with the end. Sew the same strip to the other short side and trim. Press the seam allowances toward the strips you just added. Cut the remaining length of this plaid strip in half and sew one half to each long side of the rectangle. Trim even with the ends. Sew the remaining length of this plaid strip to each long side of the rectangle and trim even with the ends. Again, press the seam allowances toward the strips you just added. Repeat this step with the other assembled rectangle, using a second 1 × 44-inch plaid strip.

7. In the same manner, using the third 1 × 44-inch plaid strip, sew a strip to two opposite sides of each mug mat square. Trim the strips even with the sides and press. Sew strips to the remaining two sides of each square; trim and press.

Assembling the Tree Place Mat

1. Referring to the photograph and the **Tree Place Mat Piecing Diagram,** sew a 2½ × 13½-inch cranberry strip to the left side of the tree rectangle. Sew the 11½ × 13½-inch cranberry rectangle to the right side of the tree rectangle. Press the seam allowances away from the appliqué section.

Tree Place Mat Piecing Diagram

2. Layer the backing piece, fleece, and place mat top; baste.

3. Machine quilt in the ditch along the outer edges of the long plaid strips. Quilt horizontal parallel lines 1 inch apart on the cranberry fabric. Do not stitch across the appliquéd section.

4. Using the 2¼-inch plaid strips, finish the outer edges with French-fold binding, mitering the corners. Instructions for making and attaching binding are on page 164.

Assembling the Bell Place Mat

1. Referring to the photograph and the **Bell Place Mat Piecing Diagram,** sew a 2½ × 13½-inch green print strip to the left side of the bell rectangle. Press the seam away from the appliqué section.

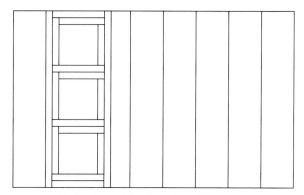

Bell Place Mat Piecing Diagram

2. Sew the 1½ × 13½-inch red print strip to the right side of the bell rectangle. Add five 2½ × 13½-inch strips to the right of the red print strip, alternating colors. Press the seams in one direction.

3. Layer the backing piece, fleece, and place mat top; baste.

4. Machine quilt in the ditch along the outer edges of the long plaid strips. Quilt in the ditch along the red and green fabric strips.

5. Using the 2¼-inch plaid strips, finish the outer edges with French-fold binding, mitering the corners. Instructions for making and attaching binding are on page 164.

Assembling the Mug Mats

1. To assemble one mug mat, place the wrong side of a plaid square atop a 5½-inch fleece square. With right sides facing, center and pin a trimmed appliqué square atop the fabric square.

2. Taking a ¼-inch seam allowance, sew around the outside of the mug mat, leaving an opening for turning. Trim the excess batting and plaid fabric even with the front of the mat.

3. Turn the mat through the opening. Hand stitch the opening closed.

4. Machine quilt around the white square.

5. Repeat Steps 1 through 4 to make the second mug mat.

Bell Appliqué Pattern

Tree Appliqué Pattern

Carnation Carousel

A swirl of appliquéd carnations lies inside a pieced octagon created by diamonds and an eight-pointed star created by triangles. Four carnations break free to fill the corners, and their appliquéd leaves overlap the pieced sections for a touch of informality. At the very heart of the wallhanging is a quilted carnation with trapunto added to make a subtle and elegant focal point.

Skill Level: Challenging

Size: Finished quilt is 41 inches square

Fabrics and Supplies

- 1¼ yards of dark green print fabric for outer border, appliqué, patchwork, and binding
- 1¼ yards of white-on-white print muslin for the center octagon, corner setting triangles, and patchwork
- ½ yard of red-and-green print fabric for framing strips, appliqué, and patchwork
- ⅓ yard of light green print fabric for appliqué and patchwork
- ¼ yard *each* of solid red, red plaid, and dark red print fabrics for appliqué and patchwork
- 1¼ yards of fabric for quilt back
- Quilt batting, larger than 41 inches square
- Rotary cutter, ruler, and mat
- Thread to match the appliqué fabrics
- Template plastic (optional)
- White acrylic yarn and blunt needle for trapunto (optional)

Cutting

The instructions are written for quick-cutting the triangles and for quick-cutting and strip-piecing the diamonds using a rotary cutter and a ruler. Note that for some of the pieces, the quick-cutting method will result in leftover strips of fabric. If you prefer to use a traditional method for cutting and piecing the triangles and diamonds, patterns for templates appear on page 145. Make templates for the appliqué pieces using the **Carnation Appliqué Diagram** on page 145. Instructions for making and using templates are on page 152.

All measurements include ¼-inch seam allowances. The measurements for the borders and the framing strips also include several extra inches in length; trim them to the exact length as they are added to the quilt top.

From the dark green print fabric, cut:
- Four 3 × 44-inch border strips
- 80 A triangles

   Quick-Cutting Method: Cut three 2⅝ × 44-inch strips. From the strips, cut forty 2⅝-inch squares. Cut each square in half diagonally to make two triangles.

- 12 C stem pieces
- Reserve the remaining fabric for binding

From the white-on-white print muslin, cut:
- One 23½-inch square for the center octagon. After the appliqué is complete, follow the instructions for trimming the square into an octagon.
- 4 corner triangles

   Quick-Cutting Method: Cut two 11⅜-inch squares. Cut each square in half diagonally to make two triangles.

- 32 B diamonds

   Quick-Cutting Method: Cut two 1¾ × 44-inch strips. Do not cut them into diamonds at this time.

From the red-and-green print fabric, cut:
- Seven 1½ × 44-inch framing strips
- 8 A triangles

   Quick-Cutting Method: Cut a 2⅝ × 44-inch strip. From the strip, cut four 2⅝-inch squares. Cut each square in half diagonally to make two triangles.

- 12 D petal pieces

From the light green print fabric, cut:
- 48 B diamonds

   Quick-Cutting Method: Cut three 1¾ × 44-inch strips. Do not cut them into diamonds at this time.

- 12 I leaf pieces
- 12 J leaf pieces

From the solid red fabric, cut:
- 16 A triangles

   Quick-Cutting Method: Cut a 2⅝ × 44-inch strip. From the strip, cut eight 2⅝-inch squares. Cut each square in half diagonally to make two triangles.

- 12 E petal pieces
- 12 F petal pieces

From the red plaid fabric, cut:
- 48 B diamonds

   Quick-Cutting Method: Cut three 1¾ × 44-inch strips. Do not cut them into diamonds at this time.

- 12 G petal pieces

From the dark red print fabric, cut:
- 24 A triangles

Quick-Cutting Method: Cut a 2⅝ × 44-inch strip. From the strip, cut twelve 2⅝-inch squares; cut each square in half diagonally to make two triangles.

■ 12 H petal pieces

Making the Center Octagon

1. Fold the muslin square in half horizontally and vertically and lightly press to find the center.

2. Using a ruler and a pencil or other removable marker, measure 7 inches out from the center point in all directions, and make small marks to form a 14-inch circle. This will act as a positioning guideline for the appliqués that make up the center wreath.

3. Refer to the **Carnation Appliqué Diagram** to see how the flower pieces are positioned in relation to one another. Using matching thread, position and appliqué the eight carnations and stems along the pencil guideline.

4. Fold the appliquéd square in half vertically and horizontally again, and lightly press to form guidelines. These guidelines will help when marking and trimming the octagon.

5. Measure and trim the square to 22½ inches.

6. On the wrong side, mark sewing lines ¼ inch to the inside of the raw edges on all four sides.

7. Referring to **Diagram 1,** measure and mark 6½ inches along each sewing line. Measure in both directions from each corner. The marks will be 4½ inches from the fold lines in the center of each side.

8. With a pencil, connect the marks to form the octagon. This line will be the sewing line. Each side of the octagon will finish 9 inches long.

9. Draw cutting lines ¼ inch to the outside of the four angled sewing lines. Trim away the corner fabric along the cutting lines.

10. Using three of the 1½ × 44-inch red-and-green print framing strips, cut eight 12-inch framing strips. With right sides together, center and sew a framing strip to each side of the octagon. Sew on the marked line, stopping the stitching ¼ inch from each end. Miter the seams at the octagon corners and trim away any excess framing strip fabric. For tips on mitering, see page 159. Press the seams toward the framing strips.

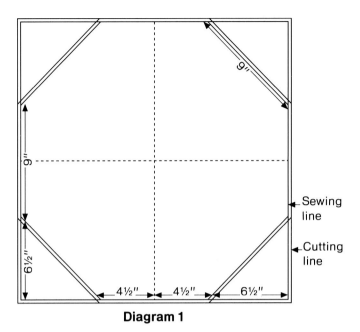

Diagram 1

Making the Triangle Units

1. Refer to the **Fabric Key** and **Diagram 2** to construct the Triangle Units. First, sew together a

Fabric Key

☐ Dark green print

▦ Dark red print

■ Solid red

☐ Red-and-green print

◩ Muslin

◪ Red plaid

■ Light green print

dark green print A triangle and a red-and-green print A triangle into a square. You will need one of these for each Triangle Unit.

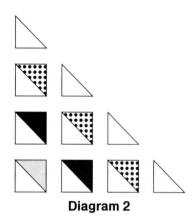

Diagram 2

2. Sew together a dark green print A triangle and a solid red A triangle into a square. You will need two of these squares for each Triangle Unit.

3. Next, sew together a dark green print A triangle and a dark red print A triangle into a square. You will need three of these squares for each Triangle Unit.

4. Referring to **Diagram 2,** sew the squares into rows and add a dark green print A triangle at the end of each row. The top row is a single dark green print triangle. Press the seams in opposite directions from row to row.

5. Join the rows, aligning the pressed seam allowances.

6. Repeat Steps 1 through 5 to make a total of eight Triangle Units.

Making the Diamond Units

1. Referring to the **Fabric Key** and **Diagram 3,** sew the 1¾ × 44-inch strips into two different strip combinations. Arrange the fabrics in the order indicated in **Diagram 3,** and offset the strips by approximately 2 inches, as shown. Press the seams in one direction.

Offset strips about 2″

Strip Set A

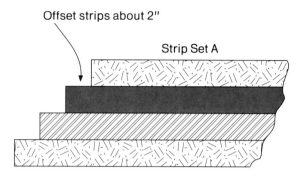

Strip Set B

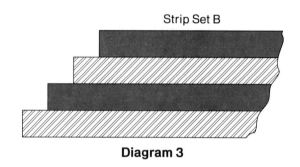

Diagram 3

2. Use a rotary cutter and a ruler with a 45 degree angle line to cut the strip sets. Place the ruler so the 45 degree angle line is parallel to the seam lines. Cut rows of diamonds, measuring 1¾ inches between the cuts as shown in **Diagram 4.** Cut 16 rows of diamonds from Strip Set A and 16 rows of diamonds from Strip Set B.

Cut strip sections 1¾″ apart

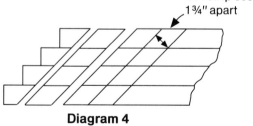

Diagram 4

3. Use four strips of diamonds, two from each Strip Set, for each Diamond Unit. Referring to **Diagram 5** for correct placement, use strips from Strip Set A for the first and fourth rows. Flip the fourth row end for end to reverse the position of the red plaid and light green print diamonds. Use strips from Strip Set B for the second and third rows. Flip the third row end for end to reverse the position of the red plaid and light green print diamonds. Sew the rows together to form the large Diamond Unit. Press. Make a total of eight Diamond Units.

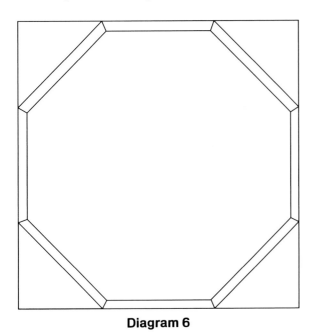

Diagram 5

Assembling the Quilt Top

1. Sew a Triangle Unit to four alternate sides of the center octagon, squaring it off as shown in **Diagram 6.** Press the seams toward the framing strips. The quilt top should measure approximately 24½ inches square, including seam allowances.

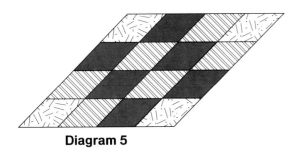

Diagram 6

2. Sew a Diamond Unit to each short side of a Triangle Unit to form a Diamond/Triangle Unit, as shown in **Diagram 7.** Press the seams toward the Triangle Unit. Make four of these Diamond/Triangle Units.

Diamond unit   Triangle unit   Diamond unit

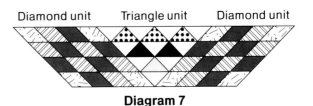

Diagram 7

3. Sew a Diamond/Triangle Unit to two opposite sides of the quilt top. Sew the two remaining units to the two remaining sides of the quilt top. Press the seams away from the center of the quilt.

4. From the four remaining 1½ × 44-inch red-and-green print strips, cut eight 17-inch framing strips. With right sides together, center and sew a framing strip on each side of the octagon, stopping the stitching ¼ inch from each end. Miter the seams at the octagon corners and trim away the excess framing strip fabric. Press the seams toward the framing strips.

Adding the Outer Corners and Border

1. Referring to the photograph for placement, appliqué a stem and carnation to each of the four muslin corner triangles. Position the appliqués so that the base of the stem will be sewn into the seam allowance when the triangle is added to the quilt top. Do not appliqué the J leaf at this time. Leave open the outside edge of the E petal so that the end of the J leaf can be inserted later.

2. Sew the appliquéd triangles to four sides of the octagon, squaring off the quilt top, as shown in the **Quilt Diagram.** Press the seams toward the framing strips. The quilt top should measure approximately 36½ inches, including seam allowances.

3. Position and appliqué the J leaf so that it overlaps the framing strip. Finish the outside edge of the E petal.

4. Add the dark green print outer border strips, mitering the border corners. Press the seams toward the borders. Instructions on adding and mitering borders are on page 159.

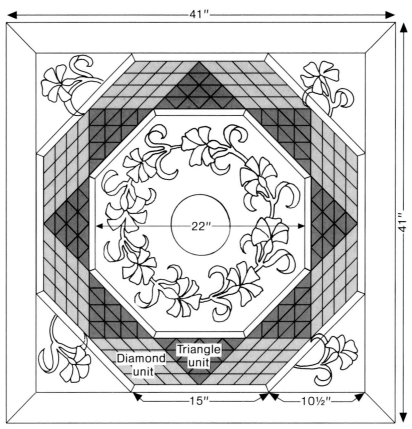

Quilt Diagram

Quilting and Finishing

1. Mark quilting designs as desired. The quilt shown has a 6-inch trapunto circle with a trapunto carnation and stipple quilting inside the circle. For more information and instructions on stipple quilting, see "Stipple Quilting for Added Texture." Use the **Carnation Appliqué Diagram** as a pattern for the quilting design. There is an arch pattern along the sides of the central octagon and in the corner triangles, and there is diagonal grid background quilting in the muslin areas. The diamonds and triangles have rows of straight-line quilting approximately ¼ inch apart. The border is quilted with a scallop pattern and diagonal grid. The appliqué pieces are outline-quilted in the ditch.

2. Layer the backing, batting, and quilt top; baste.

3. Quilt, and add trapunto work if desired. Instructions for trapunto are in "Adding Trapunto for Extra Elegance" on page 24.

4. Use the remaining dark green fabric to make French-fold binding. You will need approximately 171 inches (4¾ yards) of binding. See page 164 for instructions on making and attaching binding, and page 167 for instructions on making a hanging sleeve.

STIPPLE QUILTING FOR ADDED TEXTURE

Stippling refers to closely spaced lines of quilting, usually in background areas. Though hand stippling is very time consuming, it adds beautiful texture to a finished quilt, raising the appliqué or other quilted motifs by flattening the areas around them. Generally, stippling done by hand quilting outlines major motifs in echo-like rings. The quilting thread closely matches the background fabric.

On this quilt, the quiltmaker stippled around the central quilted carnation for a stunning effect. To create the same look in your own quilt, after quilting in the ditch next to the motif, continue to outline the shape, adding each row of stitches ⅛ to 3/16 inch away from the previous row. As the stippled area becomes flatter, stitches are apt to loosen, so be sure to keep your stitches snug as you quilt.

Two other quilts in the book also contain stippling. The Lilies of the Field quilt (page 107) has very close background cross-hatching, a variation of stipple quilting. And the Countryside Wreath quilt (page 146) contains a machine-quilted form of stippling. ◆

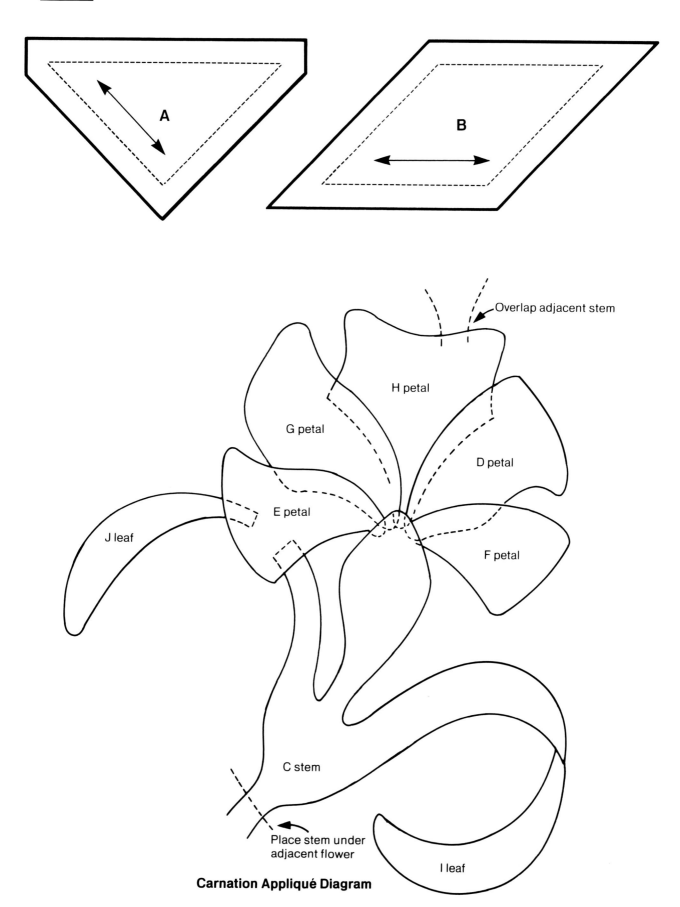

Carnation Appliqué Diagram

Countryside Wreath

A quilter's holiday wish come true! Here's a pretty pieced wreath for the wall that's easy and quick. With your rotary cutter to speed the cutting and your sewing machine to speed the quilting, you'll be able to make one for your mantel and one for a special gift.

Skill Level: Easy

Size: Finished quilt is 40 inches square
Finished block is 22 inches square

Fabrics and Supplies

- 1½ yards of cream-and-black print fabric for background and borders
- ¾ yard of dark red print fabric for block, borders, and binding
- ⅛ yard (or scraps) *each* of approximately seven dark green print fabrics for block
- 1¼ yards of fabric for quilt back
- Quilt batting, larger than 40 inches square
- Rotary cutter, ruler, and mat

Cutting

All measurements include ¼-inch seam allowances. Measurements for the borders are longer than needed; trim them to the exact length as they are added to the quilt top. Instructions are given for quick-cutting some of the pieces using a rotary cutter and a ruler. Note that for some of the pieces, the quick-cutting method will result in leftover strips of fabric.

From the cream-and-black print fabric, cut:

- Four 5½ × 44-inch outer border strips
- Four 2½ × 44-inch inner border strips
- Five 6½-inch squares

  Quick-Cutting Method: Cut a 6½ × 44-inch strip. From this strip, cut five 6½-inch squares.

- Sixteen 2½-inch squares

  Quick-Cutting Method: Cut a 2½ × 44-inch strip. From this strip, cut sixteen 2½-inch squares.

- 16 triangles

  Quick-Cutting Method: Cut a 2⅞ × 44-inch strip. From this strip, cut eight 2⅞-inch squares. Cut each square in half diagonally to make two triangles.

From the dark red print fabric, cut:

- Four 2½ × 44-inch middle border strips
- Six 2½-inch squares
- 8 triangles

  Quick-Cutting Method: Cut a 2⅞ × 44-inch strip. From this strip, cut four 2⅞-inch

squares. Cut each square in half diagonally to make two triangles.

- Reserve the remaining fabric for binding

From the dark green print fabrics, cut a total of:

- Twenty-two 2½-inch squares

  Quick-Cutting Method: Cut two 2½ × 44-inch strips. From these strips, cut twenty-two 2½-inch squares.

- 40 triangles

  Quick-Cutting Method: Cut two 2⅞ × 44-inch strips. From these strips, cut twenty 2⅞-inch squares. Cut each square in half diagonally to make two triangles.

Piecing the Sections

1. You will need three Wreath Sections, a Bow Section, and a Center Section to complete the block. To make a Wreath Section, sew together a cream triangle and a green triangle to make a square; repeat to make a total of four. In the same manner, sew together two different green triangles to make a square; repeat to make a total of two. Referring to the **Fabric Key** and **Diagram 1,** combine cream squares, green squares, and pieced squares together into rows, making sure the triangles are positioned correctly. Press the seams in opposite directions from row to row. Join the rows. Make three of these wreath units.

Fabric Key

☐ Cream print

▨ Green prints

■ Red print

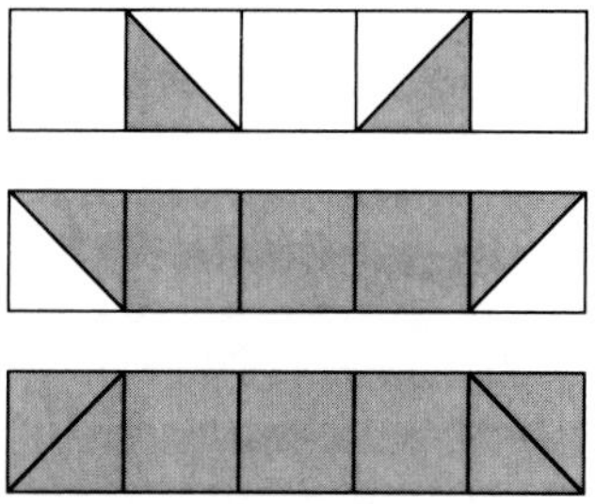

Diagram 1
Wreath Section

2. To make the Bow Section, sew together red and cream triangles into squares; repeat to make a total of four squares. In the same manner, make four red and green pieced squares. Combine red squares, cream squares, green squares, and the pieced squares into rows as shown in **Diagram 2,** making sure the triangles are positioned correctly. Press the seams in opposite directions from row to row. Join the rows.

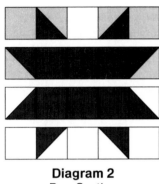

Diagram 2
Bow Section

3. To make the Center Section, make six pieced squares from green triangles. Combine two of these squares with a cream square in a row; make two of these rows. Sew one of these rows to each side of a 6½-inch cream square, as shown in **Diagram 3,** to make a center unit. Combine two pieced green squares with two solid green squares and a cream square to make a row, as shown in **Diagram 3.** Sew the row to one long side of the center unit.

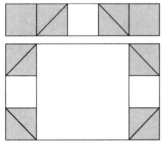

Diagram 3
Center Section

Assembling the Block

1. Sew a 6½-inch cream square to each short side of two of the pieced Wreath Sections. Press the seams toward the cream squares.

2. Referring to the **Block Assembly Diagram,** sew the third Wreath Section to the top of the Center Section. Sew the Bow Section to the bottom of the Center Section, again referring to the **Block Assembly Diagram** for correct placement.

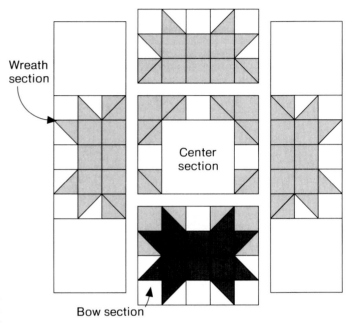

Block Assembly Diagram

3. Sew a Wreath Section to each side of the Center Section.

Adding the Borders

1. Measure the completed quilt block from left to right through the middle to determine the length of the top and bottom borders. Trim two 2½-inch-wide cream border strips to fit your block. Referring to the **Quilt Diagram** as needed, sew the strips to the top and bottom edges of the block. Press the seams toward the borders.

2. Measure the block from top to bottom through the middle, including the top and bottom border strips. Trim the remaining 2½-inch-wide cream border strips to length. Add the borders to the left and right sides of the block. Press the seams toward the borders.

3. In the same manner, add the 2½-inch-wide red border strips to the block, adding the top and bottom strips first, then the side strips. Press the seams toward the borders.

4. Referring to the **Quilt Diagram,** measure, trim, and sew the 5½-inch-wide cream outer border strips to the quilt top. Press the seams toward the borders.

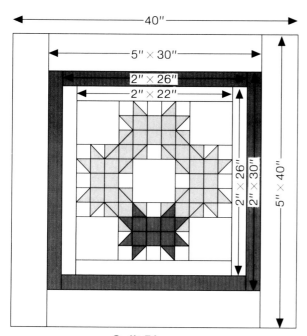

Quilt Diagram

Quilting and Finishing

1. Mark quilting designs as desired. The quilt shown was machine quilted. It has star flower motifs in the large background squares of the wreath block, with meandering machine stippling around these motifs and on the wreath patchwork. The red borders have a cable design and the outer borders have a running feather.

2. Layer the quilt top, batting, and quilt back; baste.

3. Hand or machine quilt all marked designs. For how-to on machine stippling, see "Machine Stipple Quilting."

4. Make French-fold binding from the remaining red fabric. You will need approximately 175 inches (about 4⅞ yards) of binding. See page 164 for instructions on making and attaching binding. Add a hanging sleeve, as described on page 167.

MACHINE STIPPLE QUILTING

Stipple quilting is closely spaced quilting that flattens the background areas of the quilt, making other quilting designs stand out more and almost appear stuffed. Adding the amount of quilting necessary to achieve a stippled effect is extremely time-consuming by hand, but relatively quick and easy by machine.

A random, closely spaced arrangement of meandering lines, like the example shown below, is the most popular design for machine stippling. The pattern is not marked, but rather stitched "by eye" using free-motion machine quilting techniques, as described on page 163. As you "doodle" on the machine, try to keep the random lines from crossing or touching each other.

Two other quilts in the book also contain stippling. The Lilies of the Field quilt (page 107) has very close background cross-hatching, a variation of stipple quilting. And the Carnation Carousel quilt (page 139) contains stunning hand stippling. ◆

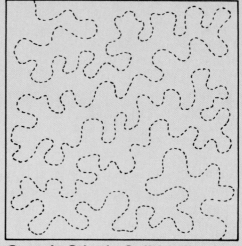

Sample Stipple Quilting Design

Tips and Techniques

In this chapter you'll find detailed descriptions of general quiltmaking techniques, as well as hints and tips designed to make your quiltmaking successful and fun. Take a few moments to read this chapter from start to finish and become familiar with what's here. Not only will you find it easier to complete the projects in this book but you'll also learn some helpful pointers that can apply to any quilt you are making.

Supplies to Have on Hand

"Quiltmaking Basics" below describes the supplies you'll need to get started on the projects in this book. "Quiltmaking Time-Savers" describes quilting tools that you may want to work with. They are readily available at quilt shops and fabric stores, and through mail-order catalogs. A few of the projects also require specialized supplies; those supplies are listed with the projects.

Quiltmaking Basics

- **Needles.** Use *sharps* for hand sewing and appliqué, and *betweens* for hand quilting. For both sharps and betweens, the larger the number, the smaller the needle. The general rule is to start with the larger-size needles and move to the smaller ones as you gain experience. Experiment with different sizes to see which are most comfortable in your hand and are the easiest to manipulate through the fabric.

- **Straight pins.** Do not use pins that have become burred or rusted; they may leave marks in your fabric. Long (1½-inch) pins with glass or plastic heads are easy to work with, especially when pinning layers.

- **Scissors.** If you are cutting your fabric with scissors, use a good, sharp pair of dressmaker's shears. Use these only on fabric. You should also have a pair of small, sharp embroidery scissors for trimming threads and seam allowances, and a pair of general scissors for cutting paper and template plastic.

- **Iron and ironing board.** Careful pressing is important for accurate piecing. To save steps and increase efficiency, keep your ironing board and iron close to your sewing area.

- **Sewing machine.** Keep it clean and in good working order.

- **Thread.** Use good quality thread for sewing, either 100 percent cotton or cotton-covered polyester. For quilting, use special quilting thread.

Quiltmaking Time-Savers

- **Rotary cutter and cutting mat.** For greater speed and accuracy, you can cut all border strips and many other pieces with a rotary cutter instead of scissors. You must always use a specially designed cutting mat when working with a rotary cutter. The self-healing surface of the mat protects the work surface and helps to grip the fabric to keep it from slipping. An all-purpose cutting mat size is 18 × 24 inches. See the section on rotary cutting on page 152 for tips on using the cutter.

- **See-through ruler.** The companion to the rotary cutter and mat is the see-through plastic ruler. These come in several sizes and shapes; a useful size to have on hand is a 6 × 24-inch heavy duty ruler that is marked in inches, quarter-inches, and eighth-inches and has a 45 degree angle line for mitering. Also handy is a ruled plastic square, 12 × 12 inches or larger.

- **Template plastic or cardboard.** Templates are rigid master patterns used to mark patchwork and appliqué shapes on fabric. Thin, semi-transparent plastic, available in sheets at quilt and craft shops, is ideal, although poster-weight cardboard can also be used for templates.

- **Plastic-coated freezer paper.** Quilters have discovered many handy uses for this type of paper, which is stocked in grocery stores with other food-wrapping supplies. Choose a quality brand, such as Reynolds.

About Fabric

Since fabric is the most essential element in a quilt, what you buy and how you treat it are important considerations. Buy the best that you can afford; you'll be far happier with the results if you work with good-quality materials. Read through this section for additional tips on selecting and preparing fabric.

Selecting Fabrics

The instructions for each of the quilts in this book include the amount of fabric you will need. When choosing fabrics, most experienced quilters insist on 100 percent cotton broadcloth, or dress-weight, fabric. It presses well and handles easily, whether you are sewing by hand or machine.

If there is a quilt specialty shop in your area, the sales staff there can help you choose fabrics. Most home sewing stores also have a section of all-cotton fabrics for quilters. If you have scraps left over from other sewing, use them only if they are all-cotton and all of similar weight.

COLOR CONFIDENCE

Deciding on a color scheme and choosing the fabrics can seem daunting to a beginner. You can take some of the mystery out of the process by learning the basics of color theory. Consult books on color theory, or seek out a class at a local quilt shop or quilt conference. Learn how helpful a color wheel can be, and understand the importance of value and scale. Your color confidence will grow as you learn the basics and then experiment with different combinations. ❖

Purchasing Fabrics

The yardages given for projects in this book are based on 44 to 45-inch-wide fabrics. These yardages are adequate for both the template and rotary-cutting methods. They have been double-checked for accuracy and always include a little extra. Be aware, however, that fabric is sometimes narrower than the size listed on the bolt, and that any quilter, no matter how experienced, can make a mistake in cutting. It never hurts to buy an extra half-yard of the fabrics for your quilt, just to be safe.

PRECUT FABRICS

You can often purchase fabric in precut pieces at quilt shops and shows and through mail-order catalogs. Here's a list of common sizes and their corresponding dimensions.

⅛ yard	4½ × 44 inches
Fat eighth	9 × 22 inches
¼ yard	9 × 44 inches
Fat quarter (also called Quilter's quarter)	18 × 22 inches
⅓ yard	12 × 44 inches
½ yard	18 × 44 inches
Long half	36 × 22 inches

Preparing Fabrics

For best results, prewash, dry, and press your fabrics before using them in your quilts. Prewashing allows shrinkage to occur and removes finishes and sizing, softening the cloth and making it easier to handle. Washing also allows colors to bleed before light and dark fabrics are combined in a quilt.

FABRICS WITH FINISHES

Chintz and polished cottons are tempting choices for quilters, with their lovely, shiny finishes that can add a touch of sparkle to a project. But before you pay for fabrics with these finishes, consider whether you will be likely to launder your quilt. Washing the fabric may remove the lovely finish. Don't prewash chintz and polished cottons—save them for wallhangings or other projects that won't need to be laundered. ◆

To wash, use your automatic washer, warm water, and a mild detergent. Dry fabric on a medium setting in your dryer or outdoors on a clothesline. It's a good idea to get in the habit of washing all your fabrics as soon as you bring them home, even if you're not planning to use them right away. Then, when you are ready to use a fabric, you won't have to wonder whether it's been washed.

While prewashing is best, some quilters prefer the crispness of unwashed fabric and feel they can achieve more accurate machine-sewn patchwork by using fabric right off the bolt. Some machine-quilters like to use unwashed fabric, then wash the project after quilting and binding so the quilt looks crinkled and old-fashioned. The risk in washing after stitching is that colors may bleed.

Setting Dye When Colors Bleed

While most fabrics today are colorfast, some, especially reds and purples, may bleed. To test fabric for colorfastness, soak a scrap in warm water. If the color bleeds, set the dye by soaking the whole piece of fabric in a solution of three parts cold water to one part vinegar. Rinse the fabric two or three times in warm water. If the fabric still bleeds, do not use it in your quilt.

Cutting the Fabric

For each project in this book, the cutting instructions follow the list of fabrics and supplies. To make the book as easy to use as possible, the cutting instructions appear two ways: Quilters who prefer the traditional method of making templates and scissor-cutting individual pieces will find template sizes and guidelines. And for quilters who prefer to rotary cut, directions for a **Quick-Cutting Method** speed things along. You may want to try a combination of techniques, using scissors and templates for pattern pieces and the rotary cutter for straight pieces like borders and bindings. Experiment and see which techniques work best for you.

For some of the projects, there are no templates. In these cases, you will either measure and cut squares, triangles, and rectangles directly from the fabric, or you will be instructed to sew strips together into strip sets and then cut them into special units to combine with others.

Although rotary cutting can be faster and more accurate than cutting with scissors, it does have one disadvantage: It does not always result in the most efficient use of fabric. In some cases, the **Quick-Cutting Method** featured in the projects will result in long strips of leftover fabric. Don't think of these as wasted bits of fabric; just add these strips to your scrap bag for future projects.

Tips on Rotary Cutting

- Keep the rotary cutter out of children's reach. The blade is extremely sharp!
- Make it a habit to always slide the blade guard into place as soon as you stop cutting.
- Always cut *away* from yourself.
- Square off the end of your fabric before measuring and cutting pieces, as shown in **Diagram 1.** Place a ruled square or right-angle triangle on the fold, and place a 6 × 24-inch ruler against the side of the square. Hold the ruler in place, remove the square, and cut along the edge of the ruler. If you are left-handed, work from the other end of the fabric.

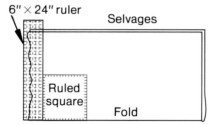

Diagram 1: Square off the uneven edges of the fabric before cutting the strips.

- When cutting strips or rectangles, cut on the crosswise grain, as shown in **Diagram 2,** unless instructed otherwise. Strips can then be cut into squares, as shown.

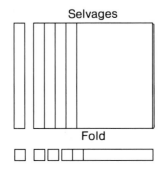

Diagram 2: Cut strips or rectangles on the crosswise grain. Cut the strips into squares.

- Check strips periodically to make sure the fabric is square and the strips are straight. Your strips should be straight, not angled. (See **Diagram 3.**) If your strips are not straight, refold the fabric, square off the edge, and begin cutting again.

Diagram 3: Check to see that the strips are straight. If they are angled, refold the fabric and square off the edge again.

- Cut triangles from squares, as shown in **Diagram 4.** The project directions will tell you whether to cut the square into two triangles by making one diagonal cut **(Diagram 4A),** or into four triangles by making two diagonal cuts **(Diagram 4B).**

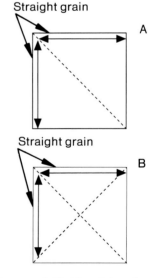

Diagram 4: Cut two triangles from a square by making one diagonal cut (A). Cut four triangles from a square by making two diagonal cuts (B).

Making and Using Templates

The patterns in this book are printed full-size, with no drafting required. For many of the pieced projects, you will have the option of either making templates using the dimensions given and cutting fabric pieces individually, or using a rotary cutter to quick-cut them.

Thin, semi-transparent plastic makes excellent, durable templates. Lay the plastic over the book page, carefully trace the patterns onto the plastic, and cut them out with scissors. To make cardboard templates, transfer the patterns to tracing paper, glue the paper to the cardboard, and cut out the templates. Copy identification letters and any grain line instructions onto your templates. Always check your templates against the printed pattern for accuracy.

TOOLS FOR MARKING TEMPLATES

Fine-point, permanent felt-tip pens are excellent for marking templates. The lines don't smear and the fine point helps ensure accuracy. Regular lead pencil also works well, but the lines may not be as easy to see. Ball-point pens will also mark the plastic, but the ink can smear onto your hands or even onto your fabric, so use these with some care. ❖

The patchwork patterns in the book are printed with double lines: an inner dashed line and an outer solid line. If you intend to sew your patchwork by hand, trace the inner dashed line to make finished-size templates. If you are making your own templates, keep in mind that the dimensions given include ¼-inch seam allowances. You will need to trim off the seam allowance on each side to get the finished-size templates needed for hand piecing. Draw around the tem-

plate on the wrong side of the fabric, as shown in **Diagram 5,** leaving ½ inch between lines. The lines you draw are the sewing lines. Then mark the ¼-inch seam allowances before you cut out the fabric pieces.

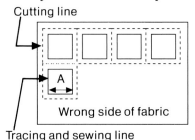

Diagram 5: If piecing by hand, mark around the template on the wrong side of the fabric. Cut it out, adding ¼-inch seam allowances on all sides.

If you plan to sew your patchwork by machine, use the outer solid line and make your templates with seam allowances included. Draw around the templates on the wrong side of the fabric, as shown in **Diagram 6.** The line you draw is the cutting line. Sew with an exact ¼-inch seam for perfect patchwork.

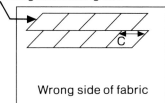

Diagram 6: If piecing by machine, use templates with seam allowances included.

Patterns for appliqué pieces are printed with only a single line. Make finished-size templates for appliqué pieces. Draw around templates on the right side of the fabric, as shown in **Diagram 7,** leaving ½ inch between pieces. The lines you draw will be your fold-under lines, or guides for turning under the edges of the appliqué pieces. Then add scant ¼-inch seam allowances as you cut out the pieces.

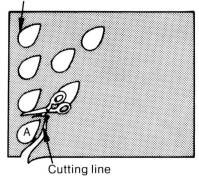

Diagram 7: Draw around the templates on the right side of the fabric for appliqué pieces. Add seam allowances as you cut out the pieces.

Tips on Piecing

The standard seam allowance for piecing is ¼ inch. For precise patchwork, where the pieces always meet exactly where they should, you must be vigilant about accurate seam allowances.

KEEPING SEAM ALLOWANCES ACCURATE

Some sewing machines come with a handy seam allowance guide marked alongside the feed dogs. On other machines, the distance from the needle to the outside of the presser foot is ¼ inch. (Measure your machine to be sure this is accurate.) On machines that have no built-in guides like these, you can create your own. Measure ¼ inch from the needle and lay down a 2-inch-long piece of masking tape. Continue to add layers of masking tape on top of the first one until you have a raised edge against which you can guide your fabric, automatically measuring the ¼-inch seam allowance. ❖

When assembling pieced blocks, keep in mind these basic rules: Combine smaller pieces to make larger units; join larger units into rows or sections; and join sections to complete the blocks. If you follow these rules, you should be able to build most blocks using only straight seams. Setting-in pieces at an angle should only be done when necessary. (Pointers on setting-in appear on the opposite page.)

Whether sewing by hand or machine, lay out the pieces for the block with right sides up, as shown in the project diagram, before you sew. For quilts with multiple blocks, cut out and piece a sample block first to make sure your fabrics work well together and to make sure you have cut out the pieces accurately.

Hand Piecing

For hand piecing, use finished-size templates to cut your fabric pieces. Join the pieces by matching marked sewing lines and securing them with pins. Sew with a running stitch from seam line to seam line, as shown in **Diagram 8,** rather than from raw edge to raw edge. As you sew, check to see that your stitching is staying on the lines, and make a backstitch every four or five stitches to reinforce and strengthen the seam. Secure the corners with an extra backstitch.

Diagram 8: Join the pieces with a running stitch, backstitching every four or five stitches.

When you cross seam allowances of previously joined smaller units, leave the seam allowances free rather than stitching them down. Make a backstitch just before you cross, slip the needle through the seam allowance, make a backstitch just after you cross, and then resume stitching the seam. (See **Diagram 9.**) When your block is finished, press the seam allowances toward the darker fabrics.

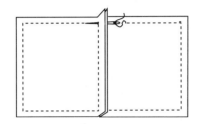

Diagram 9: When hand piecing, leave the seam allowances free by slipping through without stitching them down.

Machine Piecing

For machine piecing, cut the fabric pieces using templates with seam allowances included, or use a rotary cutter to quick-cut. Before sewing a block, sew a test seam to make sure you are taking accurate $\frac{1}{4}$-inch seams. Even $\frac{1}{16}$ inch of inaccuracy can result in a block that is not the right size. Adjust your machine to sew 10 to 12 stitches per inch. Select a neutral-color thread that blends well with the fabrics you are using.

Join the pieces by sewing from raw edge to raw edge. Press the seams before crossing them with other seams. Since the seam allowances will be stitched down when crossed with another seam, you'll need to think about the direction in which you want them to lie. Press the seam allowances toward darker fabrics whenever possible to prevent them from shadowing through lighter ones. For more information and tips on pressing, see page 156.

When you join blocks into rows, press the seam allowances in op-posite directions from row to row. Then, when you join the rows, butt the pressed seam allowances together to produce precise intersections.

In many quilts, you need to sew a large number of the same size or shape pieces together to create units for the blocks. For a bed-size quilt, this can mean a hundred or more squares, triangles, or rectangles that need to be stitched together. A timesaving method known as assembly-line piecing can reduce the drudgery. Run pairs of pieces or units through the sewing machine one after another without cutting the thread, as shown in **Diagram 10.** Once all the units you need have been sewn, snip them apart and press. You can continue to add on more pieces to these units, assembly-line fashion, until the sections are the size you need.

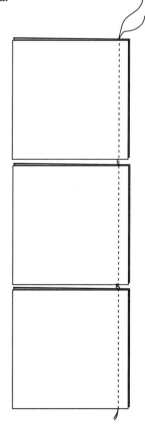

Diagram 10: Feed the units through the machine without cutting the thread.

Setting-In Pieces

Not all patchwork patterns can be assembled with continuous straight seams. An example is the Yankee Barter quilt on page 18 with its large central Feathered Star. The muslin squares that frame the star must be set into the angles created by the star. Setting-in calls for precise stitching as you insert pieces into angles, as shown in **Diagram 11.** In this example, pieces A, B, and C are set into the angles created by the four joined diamond pieces.

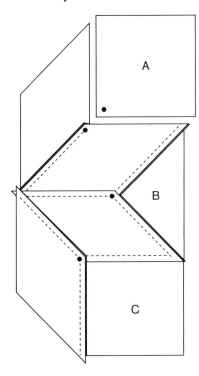

Diagram 11: Setting-in calls for careful matching of points and precise stitching. Here, pieces A, B, and C are set into the angles created by the four joined diamonds.

With hand sewing, setting-in pieces is simple. Following the directions on page 152, make finished-size templates. Trace around the templates, then mark the ¼-inch seam allowances before you cut out the pieces.

1. Pin the piece to be set in to one side of the angle, right sides

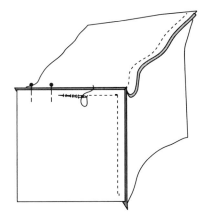

Diagram 13: Pin the adjacent edge to the other side of the angle and stitch from the corner to the outside.

STREAMLINED ASSEMBLY

For a quilt that is made of repeats of the same block (or several blocks), organize your piecing so that you do the same step for all the similar blocks at the same time. The project directions make this easy by always telling you how many units you need per block, and how many total blocks you need. ❖

---

together, matching the corners exactly.

2. Starting ¼ inch from the outside edge and working toward the corner, stitch along the seam line, as shown in **Diagram 12,** removing pins as you go. Knot the thread at the corner and clip it.

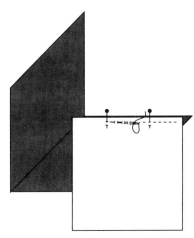

Diagram 12: Pin the pieces right sides together, and stitch from the outside into the corner.

3. Bring the adjacent edge up and pin it to the other side of the angle, as shown in **Diagram 13.** Hand stitch the seam from the corner out, stopping ¼ inch from the edge at the end of the marked seam line.

If you are setting-in pieces by machine, make special templates that will allow you to mark dots on the fabric at the points where pieces will come together. By matching dots on the pattern pieces as they meet at the angle, you can be sure of a smooth fit. To make these templates, first mark the sewing lines, then use a large needle to pierce a hole at each setting-in point. (See **Diagram 14.**) As you trace the templates onto the wrong side of the fabric, push the tip of the pencil through each of these holes to create a dot. Mark all corners of each pattern piece. You may discover later that you want to turn the piece to adjust color or pattern placement; marking all the corners allows you that option.

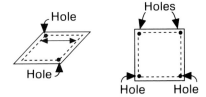

Diagram 14: For setting-in pieces by machine, make templates with holes at the setting-in points.

1. Pin a piece to one side of the angle with right sides together, matching the dots. Beginning and ending the seam with a backstitch, sew from the raw edge into the corner, and stop the stitching exactly on the marked corner dot. Don't allow any stitching to extend into the seam allowance. (See **Diagram 15.**)

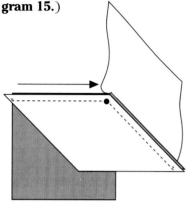

Diagram 15: Pin the piece to one side of the angle, matching dots. Stitch from the edge into the corner.

2. Remove the work from the sewing machine to realign the pieces for the other side of the seam. Swing the other side of the angled piece up, match the dots, and pin the pieces together.

3. Sew from the corner dot to the outside edge to complete the seam, again backstitching at the beginning and end. (See **Diagram 16.**) Press the seams toward the set-in piece.

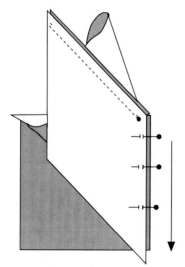

Diagram 16: Matching dots, pin the piece to the other side of the angle. Stitch from the corner out to the edge.

Pressing Basics

Proper pressing can make a big difference in the appearance of a finished block or quilt top. Quilters are divided on the issue of whether a steam or dry iron is best. Experiment to see which works best for you. For each project, pressing instructions are given as needed in the step-by-step directions. Review the list of guidelines that follow to brush up on your general pressing techniques.

■ Press a seam before crossing it with another seam.

■ Press seam allowances to one side, not open.

■ Whenever possible, press seams toward darker fabrics.

■ Press seams of adjacent rows of blocks, or rows within blocks, in opposite directions so the pressed seams will abut as the rows are joined. (See **Diagram 17.**)

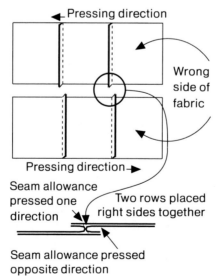

Diagram 17: Press the seams of adjacent rows in opposite directions. When the rows are placed right sides together to be joined, the pressed seams will abut.

■ Press, don't iron. Bring the iron down gently and firmly on the fabric from above,

rather than rubbing the iron over the surface of the patchwork.

■ Avoid pressing appliqués on the right side after they have been stitched to the background fabric. They are prettiest when slightly puffed, rather than flat. To press appliqués, turn the piece over and press very gently on the back side of the background fabric.

Hand Appliqué

Several of the quilts in this book include beautiful appliqué, sometimes in combination with patchwork. The true tests of fine appliqué work are smoothly turned, crisp edges and sharp points; no unsightly bumps or gaps; and nearly invisible stitches.

Depending on your personal preference, there are two popular techniques that can help you achieve flawless appliqué. In the basting-back method, as the name implies, the seam allowances are turned under and basted in place before the appliqué pieces are stitched to the background fabric. In needle-turn appliqué, the appliqué pieces are pinned in position, and the seam allowances are turned under and stitched in place as you go.

For either method, use thread that matches the appliqué pieces and stitch the appliqués to the background fabric with a blind hem or appliqué stitch, as shown in **Diagram 18.** Invest in a package of long, thin No. 11 or No. 12 needles marked *sharps.* Make stitches ⅛ inch apart or closer, and keep them snug.

When constructing appliqué blocks, always work from background to foreground. When an appliqué piece will be covered or overlapped by another, stitch the underneath piece to the background fabric first.

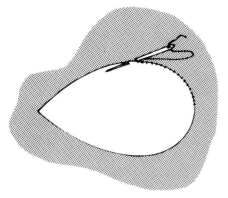

Diagram 18: Stitch the appliqués to the background with a blind hem stitch. The stitches should be nearly invisible.

Basting Back Method

1. Make finished-size cardboard or thin plastic templates. Mark around the templates on the right side of the fabric to draw fold-under lines. Draw lightly so the fold-under lines are thin.

2. Cut out the pieces, cutting a scant ¼ inch to the outside of the marked lines.

3. For each appliqué piece, turn the seam allowance under, folding along the marked line, and baste close to the fold with white or natural thread. Clip concave curves and clefts before basting. (See **Diagram 19**.) Do not baste back edges that will be covered by another appliqué.

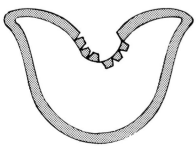

Diagram 19: Clip any concave curves, then baste back the seam allowances.

4. Pin the appliqués in place and stitch them to the background fabric. Remove the basting after the pieces are stitched down.

Needle-Turn Method

1. For this method, use plastic or cardboard templates to mark finished-size pieces. Mark lightly on the right side of the fabric.

2. Cut out the pieces, cutting a generous ⅛ inch larger than finished size.

3. Pin the pieces in position on the background fabric. Use the tip and shank of your appliqué needle to turn under ½-inch-long sections of seam allowance at a time. As you turn under a section, press it flat with your thumb and then stitch it in place.

Making Bias Strips for Stems and Vines

Fabric strips cut on the bias have more give and are easier to manipulate than strips cut on the straight grain. This makes them ideal for creating beautiful curving stems and vines and twisting ribbons. Bias strips enhance several of the projects in this book, including the Birthday Tulips (page 72) and Lilies of the Field (page 107) quilts. The instructions for the quilts include directions for cutting bias strips the proper width. Once the strips are cut, prepare them for appliqué by following the steps on page 158.

For strips that are cut ¾ inch or wider (to finish ¼ inch wide or more), prepare them by folding and steam pressing in thirds as follows.

CUTTING BIAS STRIPS

Cut bias strips with your rotary cutter using the 45 degree angle line on your see-through ruler. Straighten the left edge of your fabric, as described on page 152. Align the 45 degree angle line on your see-through ruler with the bottom edge of the fabric, as shown in **Diagram 20A,** and cut along the edge of the ruler to trim off the corner. Move the ruler across the fabric, cutting parallel strips in the needed width, as shown in **Diagram 20B.** ❖

Diagram 20: Use the 45 degree angle line on your see-through ruler to trim off the corner of the fabric (A). Then move the ruler across the fabric, cutting parallel strips of the width needed (B).

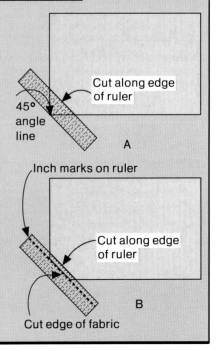

45° angle line

Cut along edge of ruler

A

Inch marks on ruler

Cut along edge of ruler

B

Cut edge of fabric

1. Place the bias strip wrong-side up on the ironing board.

2. Use the tip of the iron to fold over the first third of the fabric, as shown in **Diagram 21A.**

3. Fold over the other raw edge and press, making sure it does not extend beyond the first fold, as shown in **Diagram 21B.**

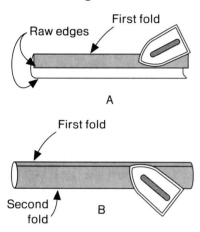

Diagram 21: Using the tip of the iron, fold over the first third and press (A). Fold over the second third and press (B), making sure the raw edge does not extend beyond the first fold.

4. Turn the strip over to the right side and press once more.

5. Baste the prepared strip in position and appliqué it in place, stitching along both folds. For curved bias strips, such as on the Birthday Tulips quilt on page 72, appliqué the inner curve first, then the outer curve.

For very thin stems or ribbons that finish ¼ inch or less, cut the bias strips slightly less than four times the finished width. For example, the strips on the Yankee Barter quilt on page 18, which are ³⁄₁₆ inch wide finished, should be cut slightly less than ¾ inch wide. Then, prepare the strips as follows.

1. Fold the strip in half, wrong sides together, and press.

USING BIAS BARS

Narrow bias strips can also be made using metal or plastic bars called bias bars or Celtic bars. These bars are available in quilt shops and mail-order catalogs. You could also make your own using thin cardboard. The bar should be equal to the required finished width of the bias strip. Center the bar on the wrong side of the fabric strip and, using the tip of your iron, fold one raw edge of the strip over the bar. Repeat with the other raw edge. Remove the bar and press the strip one more time. ❖

---

2. Fold in half again and press to form a center guideline.

3. Lightly draw a placement line on the background fabric.

4. Place the raw edges of the folded strip along the placement line. Using thread that matches the appliqué fabric, stitch the strip to the background, sewing with a small running stitch through the pressed guideline. (See **Diagram 22.**)

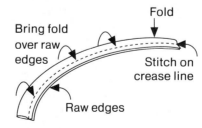

Diagram 22: Baste along the pressed guideline, then bring the folded edge over to cover the raw edges and appliqué in place.

5. Bring the folded edge over to cover the raw edges, trimming the raw edges as needed. Appliqué the fold in place.

Machine Appliqué

Machine appliqué is ideal for decorative projects and home accessories like the Calico Star Room Accessories on page 56 and the Holiday Place Mat Set on page 134. It's a quick-and-easy way to add appliqué pieces to projects that you don't want to spend time hand stitching. Plus, machine appliqué stands up well to repeated washings, so it's great for items like place mats and clothing.

Satin stitch machine appliqué can be done on any sewing machine that has a zigzag stitch setting. Use a zigzag presser foot with a channel on the bottom that will allow the heavy ridge of stitching to feed evenly. Match your thread to the appliqué pieces. Set your machine for a medium-width zigzag stitch and a very short stitch length. Test stitch on a scrap of fabric. The stitches should form a band of color and be ⅛ to ³⁄₁₆ inches wide. If necessary, loosen the top tension slightly so the top thread is barely pulled to the wrong side.

1. To prepare the appliqué pieces, use Wonder-Under or a similar paper-backed fusible webbing, following the manufacturer's instructions. For most products, the procedure is the same: Trace the appliqué shapes onto the paper side of the webbing and roughly cut out the designs, as shown in **Diagram 23.**

2. Using an iron set on wool, fuse the webbing onto the wrong side of the fabrics you have chosen for appliqués. Cut out the pieces along the tracing lines, as shown in **Diagram 24,** allowing approximately ¼ inch underlap on adjacent pieces within a design. Peel off the paper backing, position the pieces on the background fabric, and fuse in place.

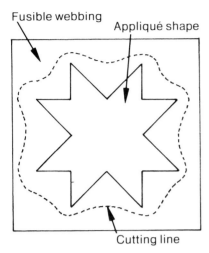

Diagram 23: *Trace the appliqué shape onto the paper side of the webbing and roughly cut out the design.*

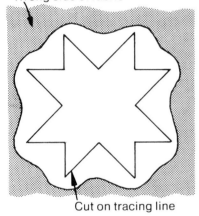

Diagram 24: *Fuse the webbing onto the wrong side of the fabric and cut along the tracing line.*

3. Stabilize the background fabric by pinning a sheet of typing paper or commercial stabilizer such as Tear-Away to the wrong side of the background fabric in the areas where you will be stitching.

4. Machine satin stitch around the edges of the appliqué pieces, covering the raw edges. Change thread colors to match the pieces. When stitching is complete, carefully tear away the stabilizer from the wrong side.

Assembling Quilt Tops

To assemble a quilt comprised of rows of blocks, such as the Amish Nine Patch (page 14), refer to the quilt diagram or photograph and lay out all the pieced or appliqué blocks, plain blocks, and setting pieces right-side up, positioned as they will be in the finished quilt.

Pin and sew the blocks together in vertical or horizontal rows for straight-set quilts, and in diagonal rows for diagonal-set quilts. Press the seams in opposite directions from row to row. Join the rows, abutting the pressed seam allowances so the intersections will be accurate.

To keep a large quilt top managable, join rows into pairs first and then join the pairs, rather than adding each row to an increasingly unwieldy top.

For the medallion-type quilt tops, such as Here Comes the Sun (page 115), follow the project instructions for constructing the quilt, generally pressing seams away from the center and toward the outer edges.

When pressing a completed top, press on the back side first, carefully clipping and removing hanging threads; then press the front, making sure all the seams are flat.

Tips for Successful Borders

For most of the quilts in this book, directions for adding the appropriate borders are included with the instructions for that quilt. Here are some general tips that can help you with any quilt you make.

- Cut borders to the desired finished width plus ½ inch for seam allowances. Always cut border strips several inches longer than needed, just to be safe. (Cutting instructions for borders in this book already include seam allowances and extra length.)

- Before adding borders, measure your completed inner quilt top. Measure through the center of the quilt rather than along the edges, which may have stretched from handling. Use this measurement to determine the exact length of your borders. This is an important step; if you don't measure first and simply give the edge of the quilt as much border as it "wants," you may end up with rippled edges on your quilt. Measuring and marking your borders first will allow you to make any necessary adjustment or ease in any fabric that may have stretched along the edge.

- Measure and mark sewing dimensions on the ends of borders before sewing them on, and wait to trim off excess fabric until after sewing.

- Fold border strips in half and press lightly or mark with a pin to indicate the halfway mark. Align this mark with the center point along the quilt side when pinning on the border.

- Press border seam allowances away from the center of the quilt.

Mitered Borders

Mitered borders add a wonderful professional touch to your quilt, and are not hard to master if you keep in mind a few basics.

1. Start by measuring your finished quilt top through the center to determine the length the borders should be.

2. If you have multiple borders that are to be mitered, find and mark the center of each border strip. Match the centers, sew the strips together, and treat them as one unit.

3. With a ruler and pencil, mark a ¼-inch sewing line along one long edge of the border strip. For a multiple border, mark the inner strip that goes next to the quilt. Fold the strip in half crosswise and press lightly to mark the halfway point.

4. Starting at the halfway point, measure out in each direction to one-half of the desired finished border length and make a mark on the sewing line.

5. Using a ruler that has a 45 degree angle line, mark the miter sewing line, as shown in **Diagram 25**, marking from the end mark made in Step 4 to the outer edge of the border strip. Mark a cutting line ¼ inch to the outside of the sewing line, but don't trim until after the border is sewn to the quilt top.

6. Pin the marked border strip to the quilt top, matching the crease at the halfway point to the center side of the quilt. Position the end marks on the border strip ¼ inch in from the raw edges of the quilt top. Repeat for all remaining border strips.

7. Stitch the borders to the quilt top, starting and stopping at the end marks exactly ¼ inch from each end. Backstitch to secure the stitching. Press the seam allowances away from the quilt top.

8. Sew the miters by folding the quilt diagonally, right sides together, and aligning the marked miter lines on adjacent borders. Stitch from the inner corner mark all the way to the outer raw edge.

9. Check the accuracy of your miter, then trim the excess seam allowance.

Quilting Designs

Exquisite quilting is often the element that makes a quilt truly special. Even a simple quilt can be set apart by the fine workmanship demonstrated by small, even stitches. While some quilts lend themselves to very simple quilting patterns, such as outline quilting, others are beautifully accented by cables, feathers, and floral designs. Suggestions for quilting designs are included with many of the project instructions. You can duplicate the design the quiltmaker used, create your own, or choose one of the many quilting templates available at quilt shops and through mail-order catalogs.

Some quilting needs no design template. Outline quilting simply follows the seams of the patchwork. It can be in the ditch, that is, right next to the seam, or it can be ¼ inch away from the seam. In-the-ditch quilting needs no marking. For ¼-inch outline quilting, you can work by eye or use ¼-inch-wide masking tape as a guide for stitching. These and other straight lines can also be marked lightly with a pencil and ruler.

Another type of quilting that needs no marking is called echo quilting. It consists of lines of quilting that outline appliqués in concentric rings or shapes. The lines are generally spaced about ½ inch apart.

In contrast to outline and echo quilting, which need no marking, quilting designs, such as the floral and geometric designs for the Miniature Iowa Amish Star quilt (page 32), should be marked before the quilt top is layered with batting and backing. How you mark depends on whether your fabric is light or dark.

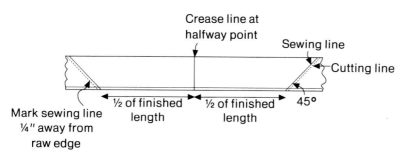

Diagram 25: Mark the border strips for mitering before sewing them to the quilt top.

CHOOSING THREAD COLOR FOR QUILTING

Most quilters choose a neutral-color thread for their quilting stitches; white and off-white are the most common. You could also choose to do your quilting in a complementary or contrasting color. The Miniature Iowa Amish Star (page 32) and Here Comes the Sun (page 115) were quilted in thread colors that match the fabrics. The colored threads blend in with the various tones. You could also choose to use a contrasting thread color. For example, if your quilt has white setting blocks alternating with pieced or appliquéd blocks, choose a color that matches one of the fabrics but contrasts with the white of the setting block. ❖

Marking Light Fabrics

If your fabric is a light color that you can see through, such as muslin, you can place the pattern under the quilt top and easily trace the quilting design onto the fabric. First, either trace the design out of the book onto good-quality tracing paper or photocopy it. If necessary, darken the lines with black fine-point permanent marker. If the pattern will be used many times, glue it to cardboard to make it sturdy. Place the pattern under the quilt top and carefully mark the designs on the fabric, making a thin, continuous line that will be covered by the quilting thread. Use a silver quilter's pencil or a mechanical pencil with thin (0.5 mm) medium (B) lead.

Marking Dark Fabrics

If you have a large enough light box and the fabric is not too dark, you may be able to trace quilting designs onto dark fabrics with the pattern underneath as described above. However, dark fabrics generally must be marked from the top with a hard-edged template and a white or silver pencil. Be sure to keep these marked lines thin.

To make simple quilting templates, trace the design onto template plastic and cut out around the outer edge. Trace around the outer edge of the template onto the fabric, then add inner lines by eye.

Quilt Backings

For each of the projects in this book, the materials list includes yardage for the quilt back. For wallhangings that are narrower than 44 inches wide, simply use a full width of yardage cut several inches longer than the quilt top. For the wider wallhangings and most of the bed quilts, the quilt backing must be pieced. For several of the large quilts, the materials list calls for 90 or 108-inch-wide fabric sold especially for quilt backing. Backings for those quilts may also be pieced if you prefer.

Whenever possible, piece quilt backings in two or three panels with the seams running parallel to the long side of the quilt. Backs for quilts such as Yankee Barter (page 18), Amish Fans and Roses (page 77), and Lilies of the Field (page 107), which are around 80 inches wide, can easily be pieced this way out of two lengths of yardage. Divide the yardage in half crosswise. Then, to avoid having a seam down the center of the quilt back, divide one of the pieces in half lengthwise. Sew a narrow panel

to each side of a full-width central panel, as shown in **Diagram 26.** Be sure to trim the selvages from the yardage before joining the panels. Press the seams away from the center of the quilt.

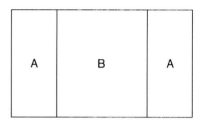

Diagram 26: Divide the yardage in half crosswise; divide one of the pieces in half lengthwise. Sew one of those halves to each side of the full-width piece, as shown.

For wider quilts, such as the Silverainbow (page 104) and the Amish Nine Patch (page 14), you may make more sensible use of your yardage by piecing the back so that the seams run parallel to the short side of the quilt, as shown in **Diagram 27.** As an example, the Amish Nine Patch quilt is $88\frac{1}{2} \times 104\frac{3}{8}$ inches. To have the seams run parallel to the long side of the quilt, you would need three panels that are each 3 yards long, for a total of 9 yards of fabric. However, if the seams run parallel to the short side of the quilt, you would need three panels that are each $2\frac{5}{8}$ yards long, for a total of approximately 8 yards of fabric.

To prepare the backing, divide the yardage crosswise into three panels. Trim the selvages and sew the full-width panels together along their long sides. In the example of the Amish Nine Patch, you would need two full-width panels and approximately one-half of the third panel, but wait to trim the third panel until after you have layered the backing with the batting and quilt top. The finished quilt backing should look like the one shown in **Diagram 27.**

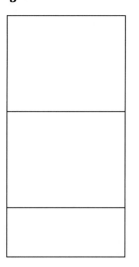

Diagram 27: Divide the yardage crosswise into three equal panels. Sew the three full-width panels together side by side. Layer the backing, batting, and quilt top with the seams running parallel to the short side of the quilt top, as shown. Trim the excess from one panel as needed.

Types of Quilt Batting

Quilters generally spend a lot of time selecting the fabrics for their quilts, but often not enough time choosing the batting they will use. When purchasing a batt for your quilt, take the time to read the manufacturer's literature and think about the intended use of your quilt. Also, talk to experienced quilters about their favorite batting. Experiment with different batts to find which type works best for you. No matter what kind you use, before layering the batting with the quilt backing and top, open the package and let the batt relax for several hours.

Polyester Batting

One hundred percent polyester batting, though lightweight, is very durable and warm. It launders without shrinking and needles easily for hand quilting. One disadvantage of polyester batting is the bearding that often occurs: The fibers migrate through the fabric of the quilt top, creating a fuzzy look. Many polyester batts are bonded, or coated, to reduce bearding. Unfortunately, the bonding makes the batting a little more difficult to needle. Polyester batting comes in many different lofts, which makes it suitable for everything from quilted clothing and home accessories to puffy, tied comforters.

Cotton Batting

All-cotton battings are popular with quilters who like a very flat, old-fashioned appearance, though some hand quilters think cotton is harder to needle. Unlike polyester, cotton fibers do not beard. At one time, all-cotton batting had to be quilted at very close intervals (¼ to ½ inch) to prevent lumping and migration of the fibers during washing. Some modern cotton batts can be laundered even when quilting is several inches apart. Note that cotton batts will shrink when washed. This is desirable for some quilters who want to create an antique look; the shrinking batt wrinkles the fabrics around the lines of quilting, instantly creating the look of an old quilt.

Cotton/Polyester Blends

Another option is a cotton/polyester blend batt, which combines the low-loft sculpted look of cotton with durability. This type of batt is easier to needle than the cotton, and can be quilted at greater intervals. The fibers are bonded, or coated, to reduce bearding. Some quilters prefer to presoak this type of batting to break down the coating and make the needling easier.

Other Options

Keep in mind, too, that batting is not the only option: For one of the quilts in this book, Amish Fans and Roses (page 77), the quiltmaker used cotton flannel as her filler, rather than batting. Quiltmakers have also used wool and silk batting.

A dark-colored batting would be a good choice for quilts with dark or black backgrounds. The dark fibers of the batting will be far less noticeable if they migrate through the quilt top than the light fibers of white batting would.

Layering and Basting

Once your quilt top is complete and marked for quilting, your batting is purchased, and your backing is prepared, you are ready to assemble and baste together the layers. Whether you plan to hand or machine quilt, the layers must be assembled securely so that the finished quilt will lie flat and smooth.

Follow the procedure below for successful layering. If you plan to quilt by hand, baste with thread. If you will be machine quilting, use safety pins. Thread basting does not hold the layers securely enough during the machine quilting process. It's also more difficult to remove when quilting is completed.

BASTING LARGE QUILTS

For best results when basting large quilts, work at two or three banquet-type tables at a community center, library, or church basement. The next best thing is a large, clear area on the living room floor. Whatever surface you work on, make sure it is completely free of dust and dirt before laying the quilt back on it. ❖

Thread Basting

1. Fold the quilt back in half lengthwise and press to form a center line. Place the back, wrong-side up, on the basting table. Position the pressed center line at the middle of the table. To keep the backing taut, use pieces of masking tape at the corners, or clamp it to the table with large binder clips from a stationery store.

2. Fold the batting in half lengthwise and lay it on the quilt backing, aligning the fold with the pressed center line. Open the batting out; smooth and pat down any wrinkles.

3. Fold the quilt top in half lengthwise, right sides together, and lay it on the batting, aligning the fold with the center of the batting. Unfold the top; smooth it out and remove any loose threads. Make sure the backing and batting are at least 2 inches larger than the quilt top on all four sides.

4. For hand quilting, use a long darning needle and white sewing thread to baste the layers together, making lines of basting approximately 4 inches apart. Baste from the center out in a radiating pattern, or make horizontal and vertical lines of basting in a lattice fashion, using the seams that join the blocks as guidelines.

Pin Basting

For machine quilting, use 1-inch-long safety pins to pin the layers together, pinning from the center out approximately every 3 inches. Be careful not to place the pins where you intend to quilt. You will need about 1,000 pins to pin baste a queen-size quilt.

Quilting

All of the full-size quilts in this book are hand quilted, but some of the smaller projects are machine quilted. The Log Cabin Purse Acces-sories (page 52), Something's Fishy (page 128), the Holiday Place Mat Set (page 134), and the Countryside Wreath wallhanging (page 146) are all machine quilted. Whether you will be stitching by hand or by machine, the tips that follow can help with your quilting.

Hand Quilting

- Use a hoop or frame to hold the quilt layers taut and smooth during quilting.
- Use short quilting needles, called *betweens,* in size 9 or 10.
- Use quilting thread rather than regular sewing thread.
- Start with a length of quilting thread about 18 inches long. This is long enough to keep you going for a while, but not so long that it tangles easily.
- Pop the knot through the fabric at the beginning and ending of each length of thread so that no knots show on the quilt front or back. To do this, insert the needle through the top and the batting about an inch away from where you will begin your quilting stitch. Bring the needle to the surface in position to make the first stitch.'Gently tug on the thread to pop the knot through the top and bury it in the batting, as shown in **Diagram 28.**

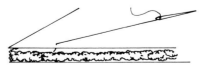

Diagram 28: Insert the needle through the top and batting, and gently tug on the thread until the knot pops through the fabric.

- Quilt by making running stitches, about ⅛ inch long, through all three layers. Try to keep the stitches straight and even.

THREAD AHEAD

For uninterrupted stitching, thread several needles with quilting thread before you begin, and keep them handy while you're working. You won't have to stop and thread a needle every time you finish a length of thread. ❖

Machine Quilting

- Use a walking foot (also called an even feed foot) on your sewing machine for quilting straight lines. Use a darning or machine embroidery foot for free-motion quilting.
- To secure the thread at the beginning and ending of a design, either backstitch or take extra short stitches.
- For free-motion quilting:

  Disengage the sewing machine feed dogs so you can manipulate the quilt freely as you quilt. (Check your sewing machine manual to see how to do this.)
  Choose continuous-line quilting designs so you won't have to lift the needle when quilting the design.
  Guide the marked design under the needle with both hands, working at an even pace so stitches will be of a consistent length.

Making and Attaching Binding

The most common edge finish for quilts is binding, cut either on the bias or on the straight of grain. Bias binding has more give, which makes it ideal for quilts which have curves or points along the outside edges. Some projects in this book are finished without binding. Directions for those finishes are included with the quilt projects.

Use the yardage reserved for binding to make the type of binding you prefer. French-fold binding, also called double-fold binding, is recommended for bed quilts. The binding strip is folded in half, and the raw edges are stitched to the edge of the quilt on the right side. The folded edge is then brought to the back side of the quilt, as shown in **Diagram 29,** and hand stitched in place. French-fold binding is easier to apply than single-fold, and

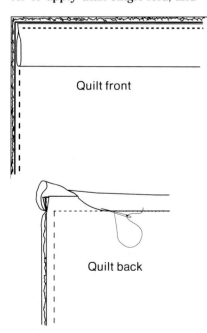

Diagram 29: For French-fold binding, fold the strip in half and stitch it to the quilt front. Bring the folded edge to the back of the quilt and hand stitch it in place.

its double thickness adds durability. The strips for this type of binding are cut four times the finished width plus seam allowances. As a general rule, cut the strips 2 inches wide for quilts with thin batting such as cotton, and 2¼ inches wide for quilts with thicker batting. The project directions in this book specify French-fold binding, and the fabric yardages are based on that type of binding.

The amount of binding needed for each project is included with the finishing instructions. Generally, you will need the perimeter of the quilt plus 10 to 12 inches for mitering corners and ending the binding. Three-fourths to one yard of fabric will usually make enough binding to finish a large quilt.

Follow the instructions below to make continuous-cut bias binding or to join straight strips for continuous straight-grain binding. Unless the project directions tell you otherwise, sew the binding to the quilt as described below, mitering the binding at the corners.

Making Continuous-Cut Bias Binding

Continuous-cut bias binding is cut in one long strip from a square of fabric that has been cut apart and resewn into a tube. You must first determine the size of the square you will need. To make approximately 400 inches of 2-inch-wide or 2¼-inch-wide French-fold binding, enough to bind most bed quilts, start with a 30-inch square. If you don't have enough fabric for one large square, use several smaller squares. To estimate the number of inches of binding a particular square will produce, use this formula:

Multiply the length of one side by the length of another side. Divide the result by the width of binding you want.

Using a 30-inch square and 2¼-inch binding as an example:

$30 \times 30 = 900 \div 2\frac{1}{4} = 400$ inches of binding.

Seven Steps to Continuous-Cut Binding

1. Once you have determined the size you need, measure and cut a square of fabric.

2. Fold the square in half diagonally and press lightly. Cut the square into two triangles, cutting on the fold line.

3. Place the two triangles, right sides together, as shown in **Diagram 30.** Sew the pieces together, taking a ¼-inch seam. Open out the two pieces and press the seam open. The resulting piece should look like the one shown in **Diagram 31.**

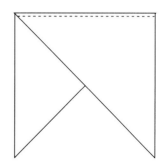

Diagram 30: Place the triangles right sides together as shown, and stitch.

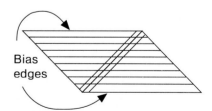

Diagram 31: Open out the two pieces and press the seam open. On the wrong side, mark cutting lines parallel to the bias edges.

4. Referring to **Diagram 31,** mark cutting lines on the wrong side of the fabric in the desired binding width. Mark parallel to the bias edges.

5. Fold the fabric, right sides together, bringing the two non-bias edges together and offsetting them by one strip width, as shown in **Diagram 32.** Pin the edges together, creating a tube, and sew, taking a ¼-inch seam. Press the seam open.

6. Cut on the marked lines, as shown in **Diagram 33,** turning the tube as you cut one long bias strip.

7. To make French-fold binding, fold the long strip in half lengthwise, wrong sides together, and press.

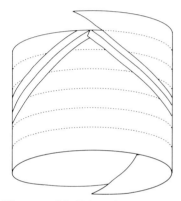

Diagram 32: Bring the non-bias edges together, offsetting them by one strip width. Sew the edges together to create a tube.

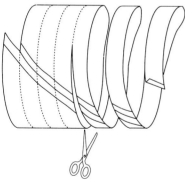

Diagram 33: Turning the tube as you go, cut along the marked lines to make one long bias strip.

Straight-Grain Binding

Straight-grain binding is a little easier to prepare than bias binding. Simply cut strips across the grain of the fabric and sew them together end to end to get the required length. Although it doesn't have the same flexibility as bias binding,

it works just fine for quilts with straight edges.

Simple Straight-Grain Binding Method

1. Refer to the project instructions for the amount of binding the quilt requires. Estimate and cut the needed number of strips. When possible, cut straight strips across the width of the fabric rather than along the length so they are slightly stretchy and easier to use.

2. Join the strips, as shown in **Diagram 34.** Place them right sides together, with each strip set in ¼ inch from the end of the other strip, as shown. Sew a diagonal seam. Trim the excess fabric, leaving a ¼-inch seam allowance. Continue adding strips until you have the length needed. For French-fold binding, fold and press the long strip in half lengthwise, wrong sides together.

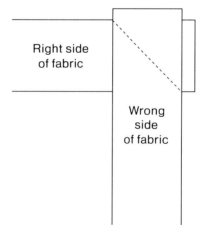

Right side of fabric

Wrong side of fabric

Diagram 34: Place the strips right sides together, positioning each strip ¼ inch in from the end of the other strip. Join with a diagonal seam.

Preparing a Quilt for Binding

Wait to trim excess batting and backing until after the binding is stitched to the top of the quilt. If the edges of the quilt are uneven after quilting, use a ruler and pencil to mark a placement line for

the binding, as close as possible to the raw edges of the quilt top. This will give you a guideline against which you can align the raw edge of the binding strip. For best results, use a ruled square to mark the placement lines at the corners.

THE BEST PRESSER FOOT

If you have a walking foot or an even feed foot for your sewing machine, use it in place of the regular presser foot when sewing on the binding. If you do not have a walking foot, thread baste around the quilt along the edges to hold the layers firmly together during binding and to avoid puckers. ❖

Attaching the Binding

1. Once you have made your binding strips (using either the continuous-cut bias or straight-grain strip method), you must prepare them so they can be attached to the quilt. Fold the long strips in half lengthwise, wrong sides together, and press.

2. Begin attaching the binding in the middle of a side, not in a corner. Place the binding strip right sides together with the quilt top, with the raw edges of the binding strip even with the raw edge of the quilt top (or the placement line if you have drawn one).

3. Fold over the beginning raw edge of the binding approximately 1 inch, as shown in **Diagram 35.** Securing the stitches with a backstitch, begin sewing ½ inch away from the fold. Sew the binding to the quilt, stitching through all layers, ¼ inch away from the raw edge of the binding.

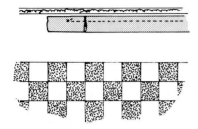

Diagram 35: Fold the raw edge back about 1 inch, and begin stitching ½ inch from the fold. Backstitch to anchor the stitching.

4. When approaching a corner, stop stitching exactly ¼ inch away from the raw edge of the corner. Backstitch and remove the quilt from the sewing machine, clipping threads.

5. Fold the binding up and away from the corner, as shown in **Diagram 36A,** forming a 45 degree angle fold.

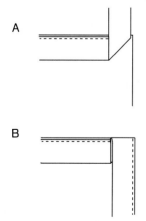

Diagram 36: Stop stitching ¼ inch from the corner and fold the binding up at a 45 degree angle (A). Fold the binding strip back down, align the raw edges with the side of the quilt top, and stitch the binding in place (B).

6. Fold the binding strip back down and align the raw edges with the adjacent side of the corner, as shown in **Diagram 36B.**

7. Begin stitching the next side at the top raw edge of the quilt, as shown in **Diagram 36B.** The fold created in the fabric is essential: it provides the fullness necessary to fit around the corners as you fold the binding to the back side of the quilt. Miter all four corners in this manner.

8. As you approach the point where you began, cross the folded-back beginning section with the ending section. Sew across the fold, as shown in **Diagram 37,** allowing the ending section to extend approximately ½ inch beyond the beginning.

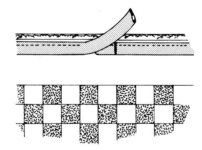

Diagram 37: Cross the beginning section with the ending section, overlapping them about ½ inch.

9. Trim away the excess batting and backing, using scissors or a rotary cutter and a ruler. Before you trim the whole quilt, trim a small section and turn the binding to the back of the quilt to determine the right amount of excess to trim. The binding will look best and wear longer if it is filled rather than hollow.

10. Turn the binding to the back of the quilt and blindstitch the folded edge in place, covering the machine stitches with the folded edge. Finish the miters at the cor-

ners by folding in the adjacent sides on the back of the quilt and placing several stitches in the miter, as shown in **Diagram 38.** Add several stitches to the miters on the front in the same manner.

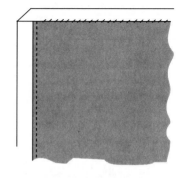

Diagram 38: Blindstitch the binding in place on the quilt back. Fold in the adjacent corner and stitch along the miter.

If you plan to add a hanging sleeve, follow the directions below to make and attach the sleeve before turning and finishing the binding.

Finishing Touches

If you are planning to display your quilt, either at home or at a quilt show, you will certainly need to add a hanging sleeve to the back. In any event, you should always sign your creation so that the generations after you who enjoy the quilt will know whose artwork it was. Follow these instructions for either or both finishes.

Making a Hanging Sleeve

The best way to prepare any of the wallhangings in this book for display is to add a hanging sleeve when you are binding the quilt. A rod or dowel can be inserted in the sleeve and supported by nails or hooks on the wall. Many quilters put hanging sleeves on bed quilts as well so that their work can be exhibited at quilt shows. Use the following procedure to add a 4-inch-wide hanging sleeve, which can accommodate a 2-inch dowel.

1. Cut a strip of muslin or other fabric that is 8½ inches wide and 1 inch shorter than the width of the finished quilt.

2. Machine hem the short ends. To hem, turn under ½ inch on each end of the strip and press. Turn under another ½ inch and stitch next to the pressed fold.

3. Fold and press the strip in half lengthwise, wrong sides together, aligning the two long raw edges.

4. Position the raw edges of the sleeve to align with the top raw edges on the back of the quilt, centering the sleeve on the quilt. The binding should already be sewn on the front, but not turned to the back of the quilt. Pin the sleeve in place.

5. Machine stitch the sleeve to the back of the quilt, stitching from the front by sewing on top of the stitches that hold the binding to the quilt.

6. Turn the binding to the back of the quilt and hand stitch it in place so that the binding covers the raw edge of the sleeve. (See **Diagram 39.**) When turning the binding on the edge that has the sleeve, you may need to trim away more batting and backing in order to turn the binding easily.

7. Hand stitch the bottom loose edge of the sleeve in place, being careful not to sew through to the front of the quilt.

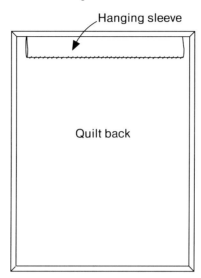

Hanging sleeve

Quilt back

Diagram 39: Stitch the raw edge of the sleeve to the top of the quilt. Bring the binding to the back of the quilt and hand stitch it in place, covering the top raw edge of the sleeve. Then, hand stitch the bottom edge of the sleeve to the quilt back.

Signing Your Quilt

Once your quilt is complete, be sure to sign and date it. If the backing is muslin, you can use a permanent pen and write the information right on the fabric. Or, you can write on a muslin label and stitch it to the back.

Some quiltmakers like to embroider their names and the date on their quilts. Others sign with short verses or dedications. If the quilt is made as a gift, you may want to note the recipient's name and the occasion. Be creative! Give your quilt the perfect finishing touch.

Directory of Quilt Shows

Because the dates and locations for many quilt shows change from year to year, and because there are new shows being added to the calendar all the time, it is impossible to provide a complete and current listing. The shows listed here are national in scope and therefore generally have fixed locations and dates. Write to the addresses provided for exact dates and complete information.

**American Quilter's Society
National Quilt Show and Contest**
Paducah, Kentucky
Date: Generally the last week in April
Mailing address:
American Quilter's Society
P.O. Box 3290
Paducah, KY 42002-3290

The Great American Quilt Festival
New York City
Date: Generally in early May
Mailing address:
Museum of American Folk Art
Quilt Connection
61 West 62nd Street
New York, NY 10023

International Quilt Festival
Houston, Texas
Date: Generally the last week in October
Mailing address:
International Quilt Festival
14520 Memorial Drive #54
Houston, TX 77079

Mid-Atlantic Quilt Festival
Williamsburg, Virginia
Date: Generally the last week in February
Mailing address:
c/o David M. & Peter J. Mancuso, Inc.
P.O. Box 667
New Hope, PA 18938

National Quilting Association
The date and location change each year for the NQA show, though it is always held during the summer.
Mailing address:
National Quilting Association
P.O. Box 393
Ellicott City, MD 21041-0393

Pacific International Quilt Festival
San Francisco, California
Date: Generally the second week in October
Mailing address:
P.I.Q.F.
c/o David M. & Peter J. Mancuso, Inc.
P.O. Box 667
New Hope, PA 18938

Quilters' Heritage Celebration
Lancaster, Pennsylvania
Date: Generally the first week in April
Mailing address:
Quilters' Heritage Celebration
P.O. Box 503
Carlinville, IL 62626

Silver Dollar City's National Quilt Festival
Branson, Missouri
Date: Generally late August or early September
Mailing address:
Special Events Department
Silver Dollar City, Inc.
West Highway 76
Branson, MO 65616